T0271349

Artificial Intelligence, Strategic Communicators and Activism

In a world that is increasingly wary of artificial intelligence (AI), this book explores the pressing need for strategic communicators to move away from being advocates for AI and move towards a more critical activist role that enables them to counter AI-driven threats to communities and relationships.

AI is contributing to inequality, misinformation and environmental damage, among other problems. This book argues that strategic communicators are uniquely placed to help counter AI-driven challenges because of their skills in relationship-building and their ability to craft and deliver messages effectively. By discussing the different professional activist approaches that communicators can take in relation to growing AI challenges, the book offers multiple perspectives that will help to build knowledge in diverse settings and develop practice, especially in community and activist strategic communication.

Research-based and combining theory with practice, this thought-provoking book will be welcomed by strategic communication scholars and practitioners alike eager to develop a critical approach to the challenges surrounding AI.

Lukasz Swiatek lectures in the School of the Arts and Media at the University of New South Wales in Sydney (Australia). He mainly undertakes research in communication and media studies, higher education, and cultural studies.

Marina Vujnovic is a professor in the Department of Communication at Monmouth University in West Long Branch, New Jersey (in the United States). Her work explores intersections between journalism and public relations, looking at issues of participation, activism, transparency, and ethics.

Chris Galloway teaches public relations on the Auckland (Aotearoa New Zealand) campus of Massey University. His research encompasses crisis communication, reputation management, and AI applications and their impacts.

Dean Kruckeberg (APR, Fellow PRSA) is a professor in the Department of Communication Studies at the University of North Carolina at Charlotte (in the United States). He is the author and co-author of many books, book chapters and articles about public relations, focusing on ethics and global public relations.

Global Public Relations Insights

This innovative series of short-form books provides a new forum to critically evaluate contemporary scholarship and global practice in all aspects of PR and communications. It aims to promote and provoke new ways of thinking, providing an opportunity to reframe public relations beyond traditional frameworks, reflecting new interpretations, emerging research, and insights from different fields. One goal of the series is to bridge the perceived gap between the "academics" and "professionals" in the PR and communications fields, and to introduce diverse voices discussing theories and practice in the global economy. The concise format (20-40,000 words) offers both new and established scholars an accessible and supportive opportunity for publishing and disseminating new ideas and emerging research.

About the Series Editor: Donnalyn Pompper is Professor, Endowed Chair in Public Relations at the University of Oregon, USA. She is the author of several books, has published extensively in peer-reviewed academic journals and also has 25 years of practical experience as a public relations manager and journalist prior to joining the academy.

Strategic Communication for Startups and Entrepreneurs in China
Linjuan Rita Men, Yi Grace Ji and Zifei Fay Chen

Public Relations as Public Diplomacy
The Royal Bank of Canada's Monthly Letter, 1943–2003
Sandra L. Braun

Public Relations and Sustainable Citizenship
Representing the Unrepresented
Debashish Munshi and Priya Kurian

Public Relations and Online Engagement
Audiences, Fandom and Influencers
Edited by Amber L. Hutchins and Natalie T.J. Tindall

Strategic Communication and AI
Public Relations with Intelligent User Interfaces
Simon Moore and Roland Hübscher

Artificial Intelligence, Strategic Communicators and Activism
Lukasz Swiatek, Marina Vujnovic, Chris Galloway and Dean Kruckeberg

For more information about this series, please visit: https://www.routledge.com/ Global-PR-Insights/book-series/GPRI

Artificial Intelligence, Strategic Communicators and Activism

Lukasz Swiatek, Marina Vujnovic, Chris Galloway and Dean Kruckeberg

Routledge
Taylor & Francis Group

LONDON AND NEW YORK

First published 2024
by Routledge
4 Park Square, Milton Park, Abingdon, Oxon OX14 4RN

and by Routledge
605 Third Avenue, New York, NY 10158

Routledge is an imprint of the Taylor & Francis Group, an informa business

British Library Cataloguing-in-Publication Data
A catalogue record for this book is available from the British Library

ISBN: 978-1-032-34826-1 (hbk)
ISBN: 978-1-032-34830-8 (pbk)
ISBN: 978-1-003-32402-7 (ebk)

DOI: 10.4324/9781003324027

Typeset in Times New Roman
by Apex CoVantage, LLC

Contents

Acknowledgements

The team at Routledge has been brilliant in helping us bring this book into being. In particular, we extend our sincere thanks to Donnalyn Pompper for all of her valuable feedback and support for the project, Jacqueline Curthoys for her thoughtfulness and guidance, Alexandra Atkinson for her care and oversight of the stages around submission, Naomi Round Cahalin for her initial production-focused support, and Manjusha Mishra for her tremendous assistance with the book in the finalisation, production and publication stages. We also extend our gratitude to the team at Apex CoVantage for all of their work during the typesetting and proofing stages; for the management of these stages, we give particular thanks to Sathyasri Kalyanasundaram.

Lukasz would like to thank the family members, friends and colleagues – too many to name individually, unfortunately – who provided encouragement and support during the writing of this book. Also, he extends his gratitude to the School of the Arts and Media, as well as the Faculty of Arts, Design and Architecture, at the University of New South Wales, for their help in enabling the research to be undertaken.

Marina would like to thank her immediate and extended family, friends and colleagues for their patience and advice. In addition, she would like to thank members of the Department of Communication at Monmouth University for their sustained support.

Chris would like to thank his writing colleagues for their collegiality, shown in a variety of much-appreciated ways.

Dean would like to thank colleagues and friends who have helped him to grow as a scholar and as an educator. Certainly significant among these are the co-authors of this volume. Others include longtime scholarly collaborators Drs. Katerina Tsetsura and Chiara Valentini. Deceased colleagues include Drs. Kenneth Starck, Douglas Ann Newsom and Judy VanSlyke Turk. Of course, nothing of significance, value and worth can be created without the support and encouragement of family.

1 Introduction

In late August 2022, Ariel Koren resigned from Google. The communication professional had been a prominent activist voice within the company and had helped advance multiple petitions calling on Google to abandon a secretive $U.S.1.2 billion military-focused artificial intelligence (AI) contract known as Project Nimbus. One of those petitions had received signatures not just from 37,500 individuals, but also from over 800 Google employees. The project, Koren had publicly asserted, had violated Google's own AI principles. She had also claimed that she had faced retaliation from the company, and had been left with no choice but to resign. In leaving Google, she wrote openly that: "Instead of listening to employees who want Google to live up to its ethical principles, Google is aggressively pursuing military contracts and stripping away the voices of its employees through a pattern of silencing and retaliation towards me and many others" (Koren in DeGeurin, 2022, para. 5). Multiple individuals and groups defended Koren following her resignation. The Alphabet Workers Union, representing employees at Google and Alphabet's other businesses, wrote: "It is the right of all Alphabet workers to voice our concerns and objections to projects like Nimbus and organise against them internally, completely free from fear of retaliation. . . . Ariel should never have faced this retaliation" (Koren in DeGeurin, 2022, para. 11).

As this anecdote shows, strategic communicators are beginning to come to terms with – and, more importantly, to take action on – the problems that AI poses, not just in their immediate vicinities, but also in broader contexts. Indeed, the world is becoming increasingly wary of AI, which is defined here (drawing on DSB, 2016; Strott et al., 2017) as an umbrella term for technologies that are capable of performing tasks that normally require human intelligence (Swiatek & Galloway, 2022). News reports and analyses about the problems connected to AI technologies are emerging week by week, oftentimes day by day. These problems include environmental damage (created,

DOI: 10.4324/9781003324027-1

among other things, by pollution, the extraction of minerals needed in the hardware, and the use of fossil fuels in the technologies), the mass capture – and, oftentimes, the misuse – of data that results in the unfair treatment of diverse populations by multiple organisations (especially companies and government agencies), the growing monopolisation of the technologies by dominant corporations, and exploitative labour practices used in the development and running of the technologies (Crawford, 2021). AI systems are neither flawless nor objective; they are also products of the imperfect arenas in which they operate more broadly. As Crawford (2021, p. 211) explains: "They [AI systems] are designed to discriminate, to amplify hierarchies, and to encode narrow classifications. When applied in social contexts such as policing, the court system, health care, and education, they can reproduce, optimize, and amplify existing structural inequalities."

The scholarship relating to AI and strategic communication, or public relations,[1] has paid little attention to the ways in which strategic communicators can help to challenge AI-driven problems (as section two of this introductory chapter outlines), due to the profession's ongoing excitement about nascent AI developments. Practitioners such as Strong (2021, para. 1) have commented that there is "reason to be optimistic" about the current technological advances, which, Yaxley (2018, p. 149) notes, enable communicators to "take advantage of opportunities where imagination and speed of response are essential". AI is already being used by strategic communicators in a range of activities, such as: media monitoring, especially in terms of finding mentions; social media engagement, through the scheduling of more targeted posts; evaluation, in providing value-adding metrics; and campaign planning, as a result of yielding richer insights about publics (Garrett, 2020).

Artificial Intelligence, Strategic Communicators and Activism argues that strategic communicators should move away from being enthusiastic, uncritical advocates of AI and, instead, become critical AI activists. This more critical role would enable them to help counter AI-driven threats to communities and relationships. Furthermore, this book argues, these professional communicators are uniquely placed to counter AI-driven threats because of their understanding of the importance of (human) relationships, their skills in relationship-building, and their ability to craft and

---

1 As Sriramesh et al. (2013) have observed, the term 'strategic communication' has increasingly been used to refer to public relations and other, similar planned communication activities. More recently, other authors – such as Braun (2020), Men et al. (2019), and Moore and Hübscher (2021) – have also discussed strategic communication and public relations (interchangeably). This book also adopts this contemporary approach.

deliver messages effectively. In the coming years, as AI continues to grow, this critical stance will only become more important given the additional dilemmas that AI will bring to individuals, organisations, communities and societies.

The Nature of AI

Although AI has ancient origins – despite often being described in ways that make it sound as though it is a recent invention – it does not yet have a widely accepted definition. Greek mythology features the earliest notions of AI – in the form of mechanical beings (essentially robots) – that also appear in stories told in ancient cultures, including those of China and Egypt (Nahodil & Vitku, 2013). The longstanding depiction of AI, in many historical texts, as an artificial humanoid servant or slave reflects humanity's persistent dream of a life of ease, realised through the delegation of cognitive and manual labour to AI (Dihal, 2020; LaGrandeur, 2011). Although fictional narratives about AI share many commonalities, scholars share no common definition of the technology. Indeed, the AGISI (2020) notes that: "Artificial Intelligence is a field of study whose major goals include its own definition." Ever since the Dartmouth Summer Research Project on Artificial Intelligence – a 1956 study meeting widely seen as the gathering that launched the modern development of AI – scholars have been attempting to develop a generally acceptable definition of the technology in connection with human intelligence. This intelligence, itself, has been viewed in many different ways over time, from "the aggregate or global capacity of the individual to act purposefully, to think rationally and to deal effectively with his [sic.] environment" (Wechsler, 1939, p. 3) to "goal-directed behaviour with adaptive value that is relevant from the human point of view" (Senior & Gyarmathy, 2021, p. 103). In this respect, discussions about human intelligence and AI in multiple fields (such as computer science, engineering, and cognitive science) question whether computer systems actually possess the potential for thought, and whether they genuinely understand their outputs and inputs, in addition to tackling topics such as the nature of human consciousness and the issue of free will (see, for example, Copeland, 2015 [1993]).

AI systems take varied forms. Frank et al. (2017) provide a useful categorisation of these systems, dividing them into three broad subsets. The first, 'narrow AI' (also termed 'applied AI' or 'weak AI'), is the most ubiquitous; it is business-focused on specific tasks, such as operating software or hardware and analysing data. The second subset, 'general AI' (also known as 'strong AI'), features the same intelligence as humans and can fluidly perform human tasks. This AI, it is thought, is decades away from being fully developed. The third subset, 'super AI', is superior in ability and intelligence to human beings, may not be able to be turned off, and may come to dominate life on Earth one day. The most significant concerns about AI often relate to this 'super' subset, even though it is only speculative at the moment.

All AI systems – narrow, general, and super – feature five key attributes, which can be understood as layers.

1. The first, top layer features machines and humans, who are the most significant element in interactions with machines.
2. The second layer, the experience layer, consists of the interfaces that people touch and see, the physical devices that they use, and the specific application that frames each experience.
3. The third layer can be described as the intelligence part of AI, because it comprises digital process logic or process software (that automates and simplifies tasks), machine intelligence (made up of algorithms and neural networks, among other resources), and software ecosystems (featuring dozens of software tools that work together).
4. The fourth layer is devoted to data and metadata, all of which are collected through the infrastructure of the Internet of Things (such as remote monitoring capabilities in household appliances and sensors in wearable devices), and are stored through systems of record or information storage systems.
5. The fifth, deepest layer is made up of infrastructure, which comprises power sources, servers, and networking, among other infrastructural components (Frank et al., 2017).

Additional approaches exist for describing and categorising AI – into, for instance, 'embodied AI' (that takes physical form) and 'non-embodied AI' (that is virtual) – but those additional approaches are not outlined here; for details, see, for example, the essay collection assembled by Lungarella et al. (2007).

Critical Insights in the Existing Scholarship

This book adds to the existing critical scholarly public relations literature about AI that has been steadily growing in recent years. In so doing, the book adds (more broadly) to the critical public relations literature, which investigates the contribution of public relations to disempowerment and mistreatment – based on race, gender, class, and other elements – as well as the problems affecting public relations itself, in challenging practitioners and academics to be "thoughtfully ethical and more egalitarian in choices of strategy, purpose, and practice" (Heath & Xifra, 2016, p. 209). Also, the book adds to wider critical AI perspectives, whose aim is to highlight and explore the growing problems surrounding AI. Crawford (2021, p. 211), writing in this critical vein, emphasises that:

> AI systems are built to see and intervene in the world in ways that primarily benefit the states, institutions, and corporations that they serve. In this sense, AI systems are expressions of power that emerge from wider economic and political forces, created to increase profits and centralize control for those who wield them.

Challenging these "expressions of power" becomes increasingly important as AI systems evolve and, without effective regulation and safeguards, come to harm growing numbers of individuals, organisations and communities.

Much of the critical public relations scholarship about AI focuses on the inequalities created or intensified by AI. Indeed, public relations – as Swiatek and Galloway (2022) comment in their outline of the "growing opportunities, questions, and concerns" relating to AI – should assume the role of interpreter to publics of both the risks and the benefits of AI, in helping practitioners and clients (as well as other parties) overcome AI-related challenges. Bourne (2019, p. 109) discusses the ways in which public relations supports AI discourses, including "promoting AI in national competitiveness and promoting 'friendly' AI to consumers, while promoting Internet inequalities". In further developing these views, Bourne and Edwards (2021) argue that the technologies used in the public relations industry can perpetuate in-built biases, as well as limit voice and diversity. Gregory and Halff (2020) examine the damage caused by Big Data-driven public relations, discussing the negative impacts on those who surrender their data and lose their agency without receiving compensation. Ardila (2020, p. IV) points out that AI technologies pose "serious reputational threats and complex ethical questions" that professionals need to address; AI's use in public relations, among other risks and disadvantages, can lead to polarisation and bias, job losses, the spreading of disinformation and misinformation, bot attacks, the unsanctioned creation of voice-fakes and deepfakes, data breaches, and invasions of privacy.

A related and larger area of scholarly research about AI in the public relations scholarship concerns ethics. The majority of the work in this area has been undertaken by the Chartered Institute of Public Relations (CIPR), thanks, in large part, to its dedicated Ethics in AI Panel. A particularly prominent source of ethics advice and commentary is the Panel's *Ethics Guide to Artificial Intelligence in PR*. In canvassing the prejudices and biases of the creators of AI systems, the guide rightly observes that: "Middle class white coders on a campus in Silicon Valley cannot foresee use cases in Blackburn, UK; Baltimore, US; or Bombay, India" (Valin & Gregory, 2020, p. 15). An ethics decision-making tree is provided in the guide to assist professionals in navigating ethical challenges; it encourages readers to: "LEARN about AI data / DEFINE the PR and AI pitfalls / IDENTIFY ethical issues and PR principles / USE [the] decision making tree / DECIDE ethically" (Valin & Gregory, 2020, p. 5). The CIPR (n.d.) has released further guides, as well as other publications, on topics ranging from "AI and data ethics" to "[t]he impacts of AI on media and PR". In a similar vein, Buhmann and White (2022) note that professional communicators need to understand the ways in which AI is used in the organisations in which they work, in addition to understanding the consequences and ethical implications of the technologies. Likewise, Swiatek et al. (2022) argue that, as AI changes ethical landscapes, professional communicators need to help:

> foster citizen participation in the development of AI ethics approaches, assist individuals and groups in navigating differing AI interests and beliefs, help mitigate reputational and compliance risks, as well as explicate AI and its implementation (and thus play an educational role).

However, the available evidence indicates that the levels of support that communication professionals can access to undertake this work is varied, because major public relations agencies and public relations professional associations offer varied amounts, and mixed types, of support relating to AI (Swiatek et al., 2022). Tilson (2017), in exploring the moral compass of public relations, also argues that AI entities and other automata challenge the field's concept of publics.

In this respect, to help enhance practitioners' understanding of AI, as well as bolster their skills in dealing with it, a growing body of scholarship is focusing on AI education and training. The topics of the studies in this area – addressing both tertiary education and continuing professional development needs – are varied. Luttrell et al. (2020) propose five considerations for addressing AI in communication education: (1) teachers should explain the ways in which traditional theory still applies to, and can be reinterpreted with, AI; (2) ethics should be a key element in education related to emerging technologies; (3) teachers should enhance their own professional development with regard to AI; (4) access to resources and partnerships should be increased, while entry barriers should be lowered; and (5) media literacy should be an essential part of communication studies. Ho (2021), in exploring AI deep learning in teaching a public relations course, has suggested that an "independent topic" curriculum might be the most effective way to help students learn about AI. Also, in terms of tertiary education, Cismaru et al. (2018) have found – from a questionnaire-based study of 98 public relations students (most aged 20 to 25) in Romania – that young adult public relations students, on the whole, have well-developed skills when it comes to digital intelligence. The professional communicator workforce, by contrast, requires more AI training and ongoing professional development. The *Asia-Pacific*

Communication Monitor 2020/21 found that "even though 75.0% of practitioners consider technology competence to be important, only 46.6% stated they have high levels of competence in relation to technology" (Macnamara et al., 2021, p. 25). Based on their study of communication professionals, López et al. (2021) recommend implementing two types of training for practitioners that target: (1) familiarity with AI tools and (2) the development of human qualities that AI cannot replicate. Zerfass et al. (2020) have found that communication managers, specifically, need to educate themselves and their teams about AI; the authors also recommend treating the implementation of AI as a leadership issue. Rahikainen (2020, p. 3) has found that informal learning – using online sources, such as blog posts – plays an important role, noting that "professionals construct their understanding of AI for PR purposes by gaining and sharing knowledge about AI, [and] acknowledging the importance and benefits of AI in PR work".

Other Insights in the Existing Scholarship

Apart from critical scholarship about AI-related harms, ethics, and education, a variety of other insights has been offered in recent years by diverse scholars, many of whom have grappled with the different ways in which AI is impacting strategic communication or public relations. Galloway and Swiatek (2018) assert that AI is "not (just) about robots", arguing that more attention needs to be paid to the wider technological, societal, and economic implications of AI for public relations. For Biswal (2020, p. 175), AI is becoming a "driving force" in the industry, while Ardila (2020) contends that it is "transforming" public relations. Scholars such as Panda et al. (2019) and Munandar and Irwansyah (2020) describe AI as a "disruption" in public relations. On that note, Soriano and Valdés (2021) – in examining automation, anticipation, and intelligence as the three key disruptive processes significantly impacting public relations in the 'fourth industrial revolution' – have proposed the creation of a 'public relations-strategic intelligence hybrid': a fusion of public relations and strategic intelligence to respond effectively to the three key disruptive processes (Soriano & Valdés, 2021).

Studies are also increasingly examining specific AI-based tools in public relations. With regard to conversational agents, Syvänen and Valentini (2020, p. 339) note that little research has been conducted into these agents, particularly chatbots, in disciplines linked to communication management; the existing research, they point out, has concentrated on chatbots at a micro level, paying much less attention to the meso (organisational) and macro (societal) levels. The authors emphasise that corporate communication scholars, especially, could contribute more to debates about stakeholder-chatbot interactions. In terms of AI-generated media releases, Suciati et al. (2021) have investigated the extent to which practitioners are prepared to accept these types of releases; their findings, from a study of Indonesian practitioners' engagement with an innovative tool for creating instant media releases, indicate that professionals generally understand and accept the perceived usefulness and ease of machine-produced releases. With regard to intelligent user interfaces, Moore and Hübscher (2021) argue that these interfaces will quickly become essential to public relations due to the advanced communication possibilities that they offer. The authors particularly urge professionals to develop an understanding of, and ready themselves for, the more personal relationships that the interfaces will foster with publics. In terms of media monitoring, Pavlik (2007) also offers a brief discussion of AI's use in news media monitoring coverage through systems that use natural language processing.

Scholars are also increasingly examining the ways in which specific populations of practitioners view, and engage with, AI. In Aotearoa New Zealand, Schutte's (2021) investigation of public relations practitioners' perspectives about emerging technologies, including AI, indicates that professionals largely support emerging technologies, often employing them in their practices, although they also have ethical concerns about the technologies. In Europe, Zerfass et al.'s (2020, p. 377) cross-national study about AI in communication management highlights that the professionals' understanding of AI is limited; the authors note that: "Lack of individual competencies and organisations struggling with different levels of competency and unclear responsibilities were identified as key challenges and risks." In Indonesia, Arief and Gustomo's (2020) investigation of public relations professionals' preparation for dealing with the impacts of AI and Big Data shows that practitioners' competencies (in relation to AI and Big Data) need to be enhanced.

Significance, Research Approach, and Scope

Artificial Intelligence, Strategic Communicators and Activism not only adds to the existing scholarly literature outlined in the previous two sections, but also provides strategic communicators with a variety of theoretical and practical tools to combat AI-driven threats. In contending that communicators can – and should – take critical approaches to AI by becoming activists supporting relationships and communities, as well as opposing harmful technologies, the book also adds to the existing scholarship about activism in the profession and field. Strategic communicators have increasingly taken a range of activist roles shaped, in different ways, by their circumstances and the unique social-change needs that they have confronted (see, for example, Demetrious, 2013; Holtzhausen, 2000, 2012; Pompper, 2015). However, as Toledano (2016, p. 280) notes in her review of the literature about public relations and activism, practitioner-activists often face competing demands in serving organisations and the public interest, finding themselves "torn between their role as advocates for the organisations they serve and their responsibilities towards the organisation's stakeholders and society at large". As such, the need to provide professionals – especially those wishing to take an 'insider-activist role' (Pompper, 2015) – with activism-focused insights and tools for combatting AI threats becomes increasingly important and urgent as AI reaches further and further into virtually every area of daily life, grows more sophisticated, and makes mistakes (as a result of programming errors) or becomes misused in the absence of effective regulation. This vital need is filled by this book.

Given the need to consider the different ways in which communication professionals can use their unique skills to confront AI threats, and given the consequent need to draw together theory relating to activism and theory about strategic communication in relation to AI, this book employs conceptual research. Specifically, following Jaakkola (2020), it uses the 'theory adaptation' approach to conceptual research. This approach concentrates on "[c]hanging the scope or perspective of an existing theory by informing it with other theories or perspectives", with a goal of enlarging the application domain of an existing theory through the introduction of a new theoretical lens (Jaakkola, 2020, p. 22). The book's focus on the specific approaches to activism that strategic communicators need to take in order to combat AI threats enlarges theory and practice about communicators' activism, thereby making a focused contribution to the critical scholarly literature relating to strategic communication or public relations and AI.

The scope of the book means that particular subjects are deliberately not covered throughout its chapters. Given the book's critical stance, the benefits of AI are not canvassed in detail, due to the focus on AI-generated harms. Consequently, the book also does not discuss the ways in which AI can be applied to the many different areas of professional communication work – ranging from media relations to crisis communication – in any detail. Broader theories and practices about social change are also not covered, as the book only focuses on activism (and, specifically, the activism that strategic communicators are realistically able to undertake within the parameters of their day-to-day work).

Outline of the Book

The remainder of the book is divided into five chapters, with the next chapter delving further into AI-driven threats that communicators are currently largely ignoring. More specifically, chapter two discusses the numerous problems, especially threats to relationships and communities, that are being generated by AI. The chapter situates its concerns about AI within the context of globally expanding neoliberal capitalism. It also considers the role being played by technology companies that currently lack sufficient regulatory oversight, and discusses the impacts of problematic AI developments on democracies. The chapter underscores the need for communication professionals to take a more critical stance towards AI technologies and to serve as critical voices, not just for their profession, but also for society at large.

In chapter three, the book's central vision – of strategic communicators becoming critical AI activists (instead of being advocates for AI) – is elaborated. This shift is necessitated by the macro- and micro-level adverse impacts being generated by the growing, under-regulated use of AI. The chapter outlines the broader need for activism in this conjuncture, details the pivot required by communication professionals to become critical AI activists, and considers the importance of the activist role in terms of the urgent need to help other publics (especially lawmakers and organisational leaders) develop guardrails to protect societies from the ever-increasing harms brought about by the use of AI.

Chapter four outlines the theoretical and practical approaches that communication professionals can use to undertake their critical AI activist work. It notes that the number and types of tasks that practitioners undertake can (and should) expand as their critical AI activities gain momentum. These tasks might include: becoming increasingly responsible for assessing the ethical ramifications of organisations' applications of specific AI technologies; helping, as necessary, to defend organisations, groups and communities from AI threats; and playing a growing part in organisational leadership to identify and neutralise AI developments that are deleterious to internal and external publics. The chapter also discusses the broader international challenges that the communicators need to take into account in their efforts.

In chapter five, the book turns to ethics: a crucial topic for strategic communication, AI and activism. The chapter canvasses some of the key ethics-related issues that communication professionals – especially in their role as critical AI activists – need to consider. In particular, the chapter discusses the importance of the professionals taking proactive, rather than reactive, approaches to ethics. It also highlights the Global Alliance for Public Relations and Communication Management as an ideal vehicle for facilitating collaboration among communication practitioners to tackle issues surrounding AI ethics.

The final chapter brings together the points made in the book about the importance of strategic communicators becoming critical AI activists (instead of continuing to be enthusiastic AI champions), especially in light of the ever-escalating problems that are being generated by AI. The chapter acknowledges, though, that communication professionals face multiple headwinds in embracing this more critical role. Numerous positive implications for organisations and governments are likely to be generated by professionals taking a more critical approach to AI, and these implications are likewise discussed. The chapter ends by suggesting avenues for further research.

References

AGISI. (2020). *A working list: Definitions of artificial intelligence and human intelligence*. AGI Sentinel Initiative. https://agisi.org/Defs_intelligence.html

Ardila, M. M. (2020). *The rise of intelligent machines: How artificial intelligence is transforming the public relations industry* [Doctoral thesis, the University of Southern California]. https://instituteforpr.org/wp-content/uploads/Manuelita-Maldonado_Publishable-Masters-Thesis_110220.pdf

Arief, N. N., & Gustomo, A. (2020). Analyzing the impact of big data and artificial intelligence on the communications profession: A case study on public relations (PR) practitioners in Indonesia. *International Journal on Advanced Science Engineering Information Technology, 10*(3), 1066–1071. https://core.ac.uk/download/pdf/325990271.pdf

Biswal, S. K. (2020). The space of artificial intelligence in public relations: The way forward. In A. Kulkarni & S. C. Satapathy (Eds.), *Optimization in machine learning and applications* (pp. 169–176). Springer. https://doi.org/10.1007/978-981-15-0994-0_11

Bourne, C. (2019). AI cheerleaders: Public relations, neoliberalism and artificial intelligence. *Public Relations Inquiry, 8*(2), 109–125. https://doi.org/10.1177/2046147X19835250

Bourne, C., & Edwards, L. (2021). 31 critical reflections on the field. In C. Valentini (Ed.), *Public relations* (pp. 601–614). De Gruyter Mouton. https://doi.org/10.1515/9783110554250-031

Braun, S. L. (2020). *Public relations as public diplomacy: The royal bank of Canada's monthly letter, 1943–2003.* Routledge. https://doi.org/10.4324/9780429323256

Buhmann, A., & White, C. L. (2022). Artificial intelligence in public relations: Role and implications. In J. H. Lipschultz, K. Freberg, & R. Luttrell (Eds.), *The Emerald handbook of computer-mediated communication and social media* (pp. 625–638). Emerald. https://doi.org/10.1108/978-1-80071-597-420221036

CIPR. (n.d.). *AI in PR guides.* Chartered Institute of Public Relations. https://www.cipr.co.uk/CIPR/Our_work/Policy/AI_in_PR_/AI_in_PR_guides.aspx

Cismaru, D. M., Gazzola, P., Ciochina, R. S., & Leovaridis, C. (2018). The rise of digital intelligence: Challenges for public relations education and practices. *Kybernetes, 47*(10), 1924–1940. https://doi.org/10.1108/K-03-2018-0145

Copeland, J. (2015 [1993]). *Artificial intelligence: A philosophical introduction.* Wiley-Blackwell.

Crawford, K. (2021). *The atlas of AI: Power, politics, and the planetary costs of artificial intelligence.* Yale University Press. https://doi.org/10.12987/9780300252392

DeGeurin, M. (2022, August 31). Google worker claims she was forced to resign after speaking out against secretive Israeli AI contract. *Gizmodo.* https://www.gizmodo.com.au/2022/08/google-worker-claims-she-was-forced-to-resign-after-speaking-out-against-secretive-israeli-ai-contract/

Demetrious, K. (2013). *Public relations, activism, and social change: Speaking up.* Routledge. https://doi.org/10.4324/9780203078440

Dihal, K. (2020). Enslaved minds: Artificial intelligence, slavery, and revolt. In S. Cave, K. Dihal, & S. Dillon (Eds.), *AI narratives: A history of imaginative thinking about intelligent machines* (pp. 189–212). Oxford University Press. https://doi.org/10.1093/oso/9780198846666.003.0009

DSB. (2016). *Defense science board summer study on autonomy.* Defense Science Board. https://www.hsdl.org/c/abstract/?docid=794641

Frank, M., Roehrig, P., & Pring, B. (2017). *What to do when machines do everything: How to get ahead in a world of AI, algorithms, bots, and big data.* Wiley.

Galloway, C., & Swiatek, L. (2018). Public relations and artificial intelligence: It's not (just) about robots. *Public Relations Review*, *44*(5), 734–740. https://doi.org/10.1016/j.pubrev.2018.10.008

Garrett, M. (2020, May 24). What does PR Automation mean for PR pros? *Meltwater*. www.meltwater.com/en/blog/what-does-pr-automation-mean-for-pr-pros

Gregory, A., & Halff, G. (2020). The damage done by big data-driven public relations. *Public Relations Review*, *46*(2), 1–7. https://doi.org/10.1016/j.pubrev.2020.101902

Heath, R. L., & Xifra, J. (2016). What is critical about critical public relations theory? In J. L'Etang, D. McKie, N. Snow, & J. Xifra (Eds.), *The Routledge handbook of critical public relations* (pp. 200–210). Routledge. https://doi.org/10.4324/9781315852492-19

Ho, C. H. (2021). *A preliminary study of artificial intelligence deep learning amid teaching of public relations course* (pp. 539–542). Second International Conference on Education, Knowledge and Information Management (ICEKIM), Xiamen, China. https://doi.org/10.1109/ICEKIM52309.2021.00124

Holtzhausen, D. R. (2000). Postmodern values in public relations. *Journal of Public Relations Research*, *12*(1), 93–114. https://doi.org/10.1207/S1532754XJPRR1201_6

Holtzhausen, D. R. (2012). *Public relations as activism: Postmodern approaches to theory & practice*. Routledge. https://doi.org/10.4324/9780203819098

Jaakkola, E. (2020). Designing conceptual articles: Four approaches. *AMS Review*, *10*(1), 18–26. https://doi.org/10.1007/s13162-020-00161-0

LaGrandeur, K. (2011). The persistent peril of the artificial slave. *Science Fiction Studies*, *38*(2), 232–252. https://doi.org/10.5621/sciefictstud.38.2.0232

López Jiménez, E. A., & Ouariachi, T. (2021). An exploration of the impact of artificial intelligence (AI) and automation for communication professionals. *Journal of Information, Communication and Ethics in Society*, *19*(2), 249–267. https://doi.org/10.1108/JICES-03-2020-0034

Lungarella, M., Iida, F., Bongard, J., & Pfeifer, R. (2007). *50 years of artificial intelligence: Essays dedicated to the 50th anniversary of artificial intelligence*. Springer. https://doi.org/10.1007/978-3-540-77296-5

Luttrell, R., Wallace, A., McCollough, C., & Lee, J. (2020). The digital divide: Addressing artificial intelligence in communication education. *Journalism & Mass Communication Educator*, *75*(4), 470–482. https://doi.org/10.1177/1077695820925286

Macnamara, J., Lwin, M. O., Hung-Baesecke, F., & Zerfass, A. (2021). *Asia-Pacific communication monitor 2020/21: Strategic issues, competency development, ethical challenges and gender equality in the communication profession: Results of a survey in 15 countries and territories*. APACD, EUPRERA. http://www.communicationmonitor.asia/media/APCM-2020-21-Report.pdf

Men, L. R., Ji, Y. G., & Chen, Z. F. (2019). *Strategic communication for startups and entrepreneurs in China*. Routledge. https://doi.org/10.4324/9780429274268

Moore, S., & Hübscher, R. (2021). *Strategic communication and AI: Public relations with intelligent user interfaces*. Routledge. https://doi.org/10.4324/9781003111320

Munandar, D. I., & Irwansyah, I. (2020, November 12). *Artificial intelligence disruption on public relations practice: What do practitioners think about it*. ICSPS 2019, Jakarta, Indonesia. https://eudl.eu/doi/10.4108/eai.12-11-2019.2293527

Nahodil, P., & Vitku, J. (2013). How to design an autonomous creature based on original life approaches. In J. Kelemen, J. Romportl, & E. Zackova (Eds.), *Beyond artificial intelligence: Contemplations, expectations, applications* (pp. 161–180). Springer. https://doi.org/10.1007/978-3-642-34422-0_11

Panda, G., Upadhyay, A. K., & Khandelwal, K. (2019). Artificial intelligence: A strategic disruption in public relations. *Journal of Creative Communications, 14*(3), 196–213. https://doi.org/10.1177/0973258619866585

Pavlik, J. V. (2007). *Mapping the consequences of technology on public relations.* Institute for Public Relations. http://citeseerx.ist.psu.edu/viewdoc/download?doi=10.1.1.129.6285&rep=rep1&type=pdf

Pompper, D. (2015). *Corporate social responsibility, sustainability and public relations: Negotiating multiple complex challenges.* Routledge. https://doi.org/10.4324/9780203733875

Rahikainen, E. (2020). *Constructing PR professionals' understanding of AI for PR purposes: A repertoire analysis of PR professionals' blog texts* [Master's thesis]. https://jyx.jyu.fi/handle/123456789/69840

Schutte, K. (2021). *Emerging technologies: Perspectives of New Zealand public relations practitioners* [Doctoral thesis, Auckland University of Technology]. http://orapp.aut.ac.nz/handle/10292/13963

Senior, J., & Gyarmathy, É. (2021). *AI and developing human intelligence: Future learning and educational innovation.* Routledge. https://doi.org/10.4324/9780429356346

Soriano, A. S., & Valdés, R. M. T. (2021). Engaging universe 4.0: The case for forming a public relations-strategic intelligence hybrid. *Public Relations Review, 47*(2), 1–12. https://doi.org/10.1016/j.pubrev.2021.102035

Sriramesh, K., Zerfass, A., & Kim, J.-N. (2013). Introduction. In K. Sriramesh, A. Zerfass, & J.-N. Kim (Eds.), *Public relations and communication management: Current trends and emerging topics* (pp. xxxi–xxxix). Routledge. https://doi.org/10.4324/9780203079256

Strong, F. (2021, January 19). 8 Innovations in public relations technology to watch. *Public relations today.* www.publicrelationstoday.com/2021/technology/trends/?open-article-id=15299584&article-title=8-innovations-in-public-relations-technology-to-watch

Strott, E., Wendin, C., Bissell, K., Oppen, F., & Lasko, R. (2017). *The essential eight technologies.* PwC. https://www.pwc.com.au/pdf/essential-8-emerging-technologies-artificial-intelligence.pdf

Suciati, P., Maulidiyanti, M., & Wiwesa, N. R. (2021). The public relations acceptance towards press release application with artificial intelligence. *Communicare: Journal of Communication Studies, 8*(1), 20–40. https://doi.org/10.37535/101008120212

Swiatek, L., & Galloway, C. (2022). Artificial intelligence and public relations: Growing opportunities, questions, and concerns. In D. Pompper, K. R. Place, & C. Kay Weaver (Eds.), *The Routledge companion to public relations* (pp. 352–362). Routledge. https://doi.org/10.4324/9781003131700-32

Swiatek, L., Galloway, C., Vujnovic, M., & Kruckeberg, D. (2022). Artificial intelligence and changing ethical landscapes in social media and computer-mediated communication: Considering the role of communication professionals. In J. H.

Lipschultz, K. Freberg, & R. Luttrell (Eds.), *The Emerald handbook of computer-mediated communication and social media* (pp. 653–670). Emerald. https://doi.org/10.1108/978-1-80071-597-420221038

Syvänen, S., & Valentini, C. (2020). Conversational agents in online organization – stakeholder interactions: A state-of-the-art analysis and implications for further research. *Journal of Communication Management, 24*(4), 339–362. https://doi.org/10.1108/JCOM-11-2019-0145

Tilson, D. J. (2017). From the natural world to artificial intelligence: Public relations as convenantal stewardship. In B. R. Brunner (Ed.), *The moral compass of public relations* (pp. 206–222). Routledge. https://doi.org/10.4324/9781315646503

Toledano, M. (2016). Advocating for reconciliation: Public relations, activism, advocacy and dialogue. *Public Relations Inquiry, 5*(3), 277–294. https://doi.org/10.1177/2046147X16666595

Valin, J., & Gregory, A. (2020). *It is always about ethics – even more with AI.* Global Alliance for Public Relations and Communication Management. https://www.globalalliancepr.org/thoughts/2020/9/17/it-is-always-about-ethics-even-more-with-ai

Wechsler, D. (1939). *The measurement of adult intelligence.* Williams & Wilkins.

Yaxley, H. (2018). Outro. In A. Theaker & H. Yaxley (Eds.), *The public relations strategic toolkit: An essential guide to successful public relations practice* (pp. 147–150). Routledge. https://doi.org/10.4324/9781315558790-13

Zerfass, A., Hagelstein, J., & Tench, R. (2020). Artificial intelligence in communication management: A cross-national study on adoption and knowledge, impact, challenges and risks. *Journal of Communication Management, 24*(4), 377–389. https://doi.org/10.1108/JCOM-10-2019-0137

Summary

This chapter has outlined the multidimensional problems that AI is generating in numerous areas, and presented the argument that the book mounts: that strategic communicators should reconsider being uncritical advocates of AI and, instead, embrace a critical and activist role enabling them to help counter AI-driven threats to relationships and communities. These communicators are well placed to counter AI-driven threats because of their understanding of human relationships' significance, their relationship-building skills, and their long-proven ability to produce and share compelling messages. The chapter has also set out the book's scope, key frameworks (relating to AI, strategic communication, and activism in connection with strategic communication), research approach, and significance.

2 Advocating for AI-Driven Threats

At any given point in time, numerous strategic communicators around the world are supporting AI. They are doing this either tacitly (by quietly but actively making use of AI-driven software and devices) or overtly (by undertaking promotional activities for, managing the crises caused by, and engaging in relationship-building on behalf of, AI-developing Big Tech giants). The communication professionals' championing of AI is likely only to increase in the coming years; however, the problems generated by AI are likely only to increase in the coming years, too. Far from being a flawless set of technologies, AI (as chapter one noted) is a product of the imperfect spheres in which it operates (Crawford, 2021), and exacerbates those spheres' imperfections. The professionals thus find themselves in the awkward position of championing technologies that are highly problematic; in so doing, these practitioners are effectively condoning the problems that AI generates.

This chapter addresses the largely uncritical stance that strategic communicators have taken towards AI to date. It explores the issues that this stance generates not just for societies – and, in particular, communities and (human) relationships – but also for the communication profession. The chapter begins by discussing the threats to which AI is giving rise – a discussion that complements the outline of the problems presented in the introduction – with a focus on the threats to relationships and communities. After that, it examines the problems that the communicators' uncritical stance is producing for the profession. It then looks more broadly at the issues connected to the tech giants and inadequate government oversight in relation to democracy. A short conclusion offers final thoughts about the ideas discussed in the chapter.

Threats to Communities and Relationships

Reports of AI-generated problems have grown exponentially over the years. Already by 2017, the activities of AI technologies had resulted in: safety risks (especially in transportation and personal care); racism, sexism and discrimination (in terms of data processing); issues in legal decision-making; privacy concerns; and adverse impacts on hiring processes and employment

DOI: 10.4324/9781003324027-2

(Guihot et al., 2017). Since that time, these (and other) issues have only grown. As the introduction (in this book) has noted, the problems generated by AI – such as environmental damage – are manifold; they often go unnoticed in most individuals' day-to-day lives. When AI-generated issues are encountered, they most often take the form of software-related complications (such as the unwholesome recommendations offered by Snapchat's experimental chatbot, which provided one U.S. columnist with advice about hiding marijuana and alcohol, cheating on homework, and defeating parental phone controls) (Fowler, 2023). 'Runaway AI' could radically alter the ways in which our societies function and, more concerningly, harm humanity on a grand scale (Guihot et al., 2017).

AI also threatens (human) relationships and communities. As the previous paragraphs (as well as the book's introduction) have noted, damage has already been done as a result of assorted destructive activities, such as AI-enhanced discrimination, AI's offering of hazard-generating advice, the exploitation of labourers and the breaching of privacy, as well as conflicts that are being caused among employees due to organisations' controversial AI activities. All of these problems (among many others), in various ways, damage relationships between individuals and create divisions within communities. Although AI has not yet caused irrevocable or widespread damage to relationships and communities, the threats are very real, given the fact that the technologies bring with them many unforeseen, negative consequences. Weitzner (2022, para. 7) notes – in the course of writing about faulty AI autopilot software, as well as death that has resulted from self-driving car crashes – that all manner of "harms emerge in all sorts of unexpected ways". This unexpectedness makes the threats of AI all the more serious; he rightly asks: "What happens when the nefarious implications of an AI are not immediately recognized? Or when it is too difficult to take the AI offline when necessary?"

The threats are particularly worrying given the fact that relationships and communities are the essential pillars of societies. More broadly, human existence simply does not function properly without these elements of care and support. As deWit and O'Neill (2014, p. 19) note: "Each person needs to feel that she belongs or is attached to others. People need to feel cared about, and they function best if they feel a sense of community with others." No matter where they go or how high they rise in life, Roberts (2014) also observes, individuals continually return to the social relationships that are the bedrock of communities, due to the familiarity, security and stability that they offer. Vital elements for human thriving – such as empathy, warmth, and social responsibility (Crimston et al., 2016) – are developed as part of individuals' and groups' 'moral circles', of which AI is not yet a part (Crimston, 2018) and may never be a part. Moreover, international collaborations to develop AI that respects human beings and human rights are only in their initial stages (Gillwald & Adams, 2021).

Profession-related Problems

The threats being generated by AI have also not yet successfully been registered by public relations, which is changing as a profession, too. Until now, a significant amount of the scholarly work and industry commentary about AI has featured uncritical support for the implementation and use of AI by communication professionals (Galloway & Swiatek, 2018; Swiatek & Galloway, 2022). The published content encompasses both industry and agency voices that cheerlead (Bourne, 2019) the adoption of this new technology as being obviously commonsensical and for a public good. One publication identifies 20 ways in which AI could transform public relations and communication management; it lists, among other tasks, applications such as: producing news releases and media reports using natural language generation (NLG), performing advanced sentiment analysis on media clippings and social posts/comments, targeting media outlets and contacts that have the greatest probability of generating coverage (rather than using traditional manual list-building that is based on categories and keyword searches), and creating custom story angles for journalists based on their interests, past coverage, personalities, and trends (Kaput, 2021, para. 17). While the article warns that the list of tasks that AI could perform should give PR practitioners "pause" (for thought), it nevertheless identifies AI tools for public relations practitioners to explore, with only a cursory call to "understand" the tools before using them (Kaput, 2021, paras. 19 & 21). Similarly, a *PR Daily* article suggests, among other examples, predictive analytics, attribution for earned media, and speech-to-text technology as tools useful for current and future practitioners (Chittick, 2022). The article additionally poses a typical question addressing the fear that AI might end up taking the place of practitioners:

> Will AI eventually replace PR pros? A simple mindset shift can alleviate the worry. If we look for the ways technology can make us more effective by freeing us to come up with better ideas and affording us opportunities to explore those ideas, then we will rise with this wave of innovation rather than letting it overpower us.
>
> (Chittick, 2022, para. 14)

The answer that the article provides shows the futurity and optimism that Bourne (2019) notes when analysing the discourse related to the use of AI in PR.

These articles highlight an uncritical understanding, more broadly, of the real consequences that the implementation of AI entails for the white-collar professional class. Although it is true that automation has already come in handy in some aspects of professionals' work, the future of the public relations profession as we know it is entering a phase of complete restructuring, and many of its current practices will disappear. To understand the sheer scope of this restructuring, it is worth looking at the apt analysis of the decline of the professional class by Susskind and Susskind (2022) – building on their earlier work (especially Susskind & Susskind, 2018) – that provides a narrative focusing on the current global debate about the future of work. The authors' work suggests that new technologies, particularly automation, are virtually erasing what we had once known as 'practical expertise', which is their term for "knowledge, wisdom, experience, skills" (Susskind & Susskind, 2018, p. 126). More specifically, these authors argue that:

> Machines are becoming increasingly capable and are taking on more and more of the tasks that were once the exclusive province of human professionals. While new tasks will no doubt arise in years to come, machines are likely in times to come to take on many of these as well. In the medium term, during the 2020s, this will not mean unemployment for professionals. But there will be widespread redeployment and a need for extensive retraining. In the long run, however, we find it hard to avoid the conclusion that there will be a steady decline in the need for traditional flesh-and-blood professionals working as they do today.
>
> (Susskind & Susskind, 2022, p. xxv)

The decline of such professionals will have multiple (as-yet-undetermined) flow-on effects for communities and, more broadly, whole societies.

Rapidly developing technologies offer causes for both optimism and concern. The Susskinds predict two parallel processes that will continue to shape the future of professions under the pressure of technological developments. One process promises to use technology to aid the work of professionals, and to "streamline" and "optimize" their work (Susskind & Susskind, 2018, p. 125). The second process is more radical, offering the use of automation and machines, either without people or with people at their helms who are not necessarily the white-collar professionals we see today among the ranks of doctors, journalists, lawyers, educators and, of course, communication professionals. The ongoing, significant investment in technologies, the growth of Big Tech, and the reshaping of economies around the world are clearly an intentional result of the rise of neoliberalism – the theory of political economic practices proposing that "human well-being can best be advanced by liberating individual entrepreneurial freedoms and skills within an institutional framework characterized by strong private property rights, free markets, and free trade" (Harvey, 2005, p. 2) – over the decades. Neoliberal lingua franca encompasses processes such as streamlining, optimisation, and efficiency, all of which are labour cost-saving strategies that, unsurprisingly, coincide with the decline of labour organising, which grew during the global COVID-19 pandemic when isolation quickly reshaped workplaces. Another heavily neoliberal and related discourse is the discourse of deprofessionalisation.

Academics, for instance, have witnessed deprofessionalisation in the rapid attacks that have been made on the principle of shared governance; as a result, faculty expertise in curricular matters is increasingly being challenged (Vujnovic & Foster, 2022). Questioning why professions are needed is directly related to the idea that if expertise is removed from professions, the need for professionals is eliminated, ultimately resulting in a cost-saving strategy that paves the way for machines to complete tasks. Additionally, if a profession is reduced just to a set of practical skills, those skills can easily be undertaken by machines, resulting in even greater labour savings. The reduction of the cost of human labour has been the main focus of the spread of unfettered neoliberal global capitalism for decades, as well as the core of the neoliberal global agenda; at the moment, the reduction is being led by technology companies.

The concept of 'precarisation' can help to make further sense of these developments. This useful concept is offered by Maronitis (2019) in his discussion of neoliberal governance after the 2008 economic crisis. For Maronitis (2019, p. 1), this governance has been characterised by precarisation: both a "dominant mode of governing" and the "most effective means for capital accumulation". Hence, the discourse about deprofessionalisation must be viewed in the context of this new neoliberal form of governance that is characterised by constant instability, insecurity and fear. Currently, much of that fear and uncertainty rests on the implementation of AI technologies. This debate requires more analysis than can possibly be offered here, but it is an important building block in understanding the precarious conditions that all white-collar professions, including public relations, are currently facing and will face even more significantly in the future. As the Susskinds (2018, p. 126) note, the modernist idea of the professional class has also been built on the principle of exclusion, meaning that expertise has effectively served to "exclude others from large expanses of knowledge", to which professionals serve as "gatekeepers". The new technological era, however, has ushered in, under the guise of the expansion of democratic processes, new gatekeepers: Big Tech. These gatekeepers – that is, the largest technology corporations – encourage everyone to trust in them to offer the fair, democratic, well-designed and generally beautifully envisioned society of the future. The premise that everything should simply be handed over to Big Tech – and its leaders, such as Elon Musk and Mark Zuckerberg – for safekeeping is absolutely contestable, even though there is a need to re-examine the gatekeeping of knowledge and the role of the professions. Hence, it is imperative that communication professionals recognise this new reality and turn away from advocating for AI-driven threats by critically examining their professional standing in society. Additionally, these professionals, collectively, can be an important voice for other workers, and for society at large, by leading important conversations about the future of work.

The Tech Giants, Government and Democracy

The takeover of the professional discourse, and of the professions themselves, by the technology industry has dire consequences for the status of workers in societies, for policy, and ultimately for democracies. A valuable lesson, in this respect, is provided by blue-collar workers, many of whom have been grasping for a new reality for some time. The widely repeated narrative that offshoring, due to globalisation, has bled blue-collar jobs to other parts of the world is only partly accurate; these jobs have, for some time, been disappearing due more to the process of automation than to offshoring. The next class of workers now being affected by automation is the white-collar professional class. Roose (2022a, para. 1), like other analysts who are acutely aware of this phenomenon, notes that:

> For years, the conventional wisdom among Silicon Valley futurists was that artificial intelligence and automation spelled doom for blue-collar workers whose jobs involved repetitive manual labor. Truck drivers, retail cashiers and warehouse workers would all lose their jobs to robots, they said, while workers in creative fields like art, entertainment and media would be safe. Well, an unexpected thing happened recently: A.I. entered the creative class.

Concerningly, the spread of automation is not diminishing, and even more jobs (in the creative class, as well as in other classes) are likely to be automated in future.

The speed at which AI technologies have been ushered into societies – with virtually no, or little, discussion of policy adjustments or user guidelines to safeguard individuals, groups and organisations against adversarial effects – is nothing short of stunning. This development is not accidental; rather, it is by design. The widespread implementation of AI is working exactly as it should in the context of a global neoliberal economy in which "winners take all" (Giridharadas, 2018). Particularly problematic are open-source AI models. Although individuals the world over might marvel at these models' functions, especially while they are busy playing with them, these technologies are tearing into the fabric of societies and are exploiting their weakest members. Consider the following anecdote about one such open-source AI model, Stable Diffusion, and the adverse effects that it has generated.

> Already, Stable Diffusion and its open-source offshoots have been used to create plenty of offensive images (including, judging by a quick scan of Twitter, a truly astonishing amount of anime pornography). In recent days, several Reddit forums have been shut down after being inundated with nonconsensual nude images, largely made with Stable Diffusion. The company tried to rein in the chaos, telling users not to "generate anything

you'd be ashamed to show your mother," but has stopped short of setting up stricter filters. Representative Anna Eshoo, Democrat of California, recently sent a letter to federal regulators warning that people had created graphic images of "violently beaten Asian women" using Stable Diffusion. Ms. Eshoo urged regulators to crack down against "unsafe" open-source A.I. models.

(Roose, 2022b, para. 11)

The social harms resulting from the creation of such content might not be immediately apparent to everyone as they go about their day-to-day lives, but the harms are more than likely to become cumulatively apparent in the long term and have devastating, widespread consequences.

The policy challenges related to copyright and intellectual property are also concerning. One particular class action lawsuit against Microsoft is emblematic of these challenges. The lawsuit involves the Los Angeles-based programmer Matthew Butterick, who is suing Microsoft for the deployment of an AI model called Copilot that has gained its skills by analysing billions of lines of code from the Internet: code that was originally developed by programmers such as Butterick. Metz (2022) explains that:

Mr. Butterick, 52, equates this process to piracy, because the system does not acknowledge its debt to existing work. His lawsuit claims that Microsoft and its collaborators violated the legal rights of millions of programmers who spent years writing the original code. The suit is believed to be the first legal attack on a design technique called "A.I. training," which is a way of building artificial intelligence that is poised to remake the tech industry. In recent years, many artists, writers, pundits, and privacy activists have complained that companies are training their A.I. systems using data that does not belong to them.

Paradox and cruelty abound in this example, which provides an illustration of the ways in which the tech industry is training its AI models to use human work without compensating humans for that work, and ultimately aiming to use the new AI models as replacements for the human work that created them in the first place. Another example of the tech industry's unfair treatment of workers is Open AI's use of "Kenyan laborers earning less than $2 per hour" to make another open-source AI model, ChatGPT, "less toxic" (Perrigio, 2023).

Globally, it seems that societies have been caught by surprise. Governments, professional associations, corporations and various other organisations have mostly taken reactive (rather than proactive) stances at best. For example, a panel of international AI experts – including both practitioners and academics (assembled by the *MIT Sloan Management Review* and the Boston Consulting Group), tasked with discovering the ways in which responsible AI has been implemented in organisations worldwide – has found, from a global survey of more than 1,000 executives, that there is overwhelming agreement (among the executives) that AI should be implemented responsibly; however, only about half of the respondents said that it actually is, exposing "a dramatic gap between expectations and reality" (Kiron et al., 2022, para. 2).

Conclusion

Communication professionals must quickly snap out of a state of daydreaming about AI technologies as being innocuous and even "friendly" (Bourne, 2019, p. 109). The practitioners urgently need to wake up to a reality that is much more complex, even grim. The consequences of the uncritical embrace of AI – through changes to discourse, slow policy development, and reactive (rather than proactive) stances – are deep and widespread, encompassing everything from the further erosion of labour security to the deepening of inequalities online and throughout societies. Given the high stakes, communicators should be willing to raise their critical voices in the face of a technological revolution that is gathering both speed and victims. The next chapter builds on the ideas discussed in this chapter by elaborating the book's central vision: that is, of strategic communicators becoming critical AI activists helping to counter AI-driven threats.

References

Bourne, C. (2019). AI cheerleaders: Public relations, neoliberalism and artificial intelligence. *Public Relations Inquiry*, 8(2), 109–125. https://doi.org/10.1177/2046147X 19835250

Chittick, R. (2022, January 5). 7 ways artificial intelligence will change the game for PR pros. *PR Daily*. https://www.prdaily.com/7-ways-artificial-intelligence-will-change-the-game-for-pr-pros/

Crawford, K. (2021). *The atlas of AI: Power, politics, and the planetary costs of artificial intelligence*. Yale University Press. https://doi.org/10.12987/9780300252392

Crimston, C. (2018, February 22). How we decide who and what we care about – and whether robots stand a chance. *The Conversation*. https://theconversation.com/how-we-decide-who-and-what-we-care-about-and-whether-robots-stand-a-chance-91987

Crimston, D., Bain, P. G., Hornsey, M. J., & Bastian, B. (2016). Moral expansiveness: Examining variability in the extension of the moral world. *Journal of Personality and Social Psychology*, 111(4), 636–653. https://doi.org/10.1037/pspp0000086

deWit, S. C., & O'Neill, P. (2014). *Fundamental concepts and skills for nursing* (4th ed.). Elsevier.

Fowler, G. A. (2023, March 15). Snapchat tried to make a safe AI: It chats with me about booze and sex. *The Washington Post*. https://www.washingtonpost.com/technology/2023/03/14/snapchat-myai/

Galloway, C., & Swiatek, L. (2018). Public relations and artificial intelligence: It's not (just) about robots. *Public Relations Review, 44*(5), 734–740. https://doi.org/10.1016/j.pubrev.2018.10.008

Gillwald, A., & Adams, R. (2021, December 7). Artificial intelligence carries a huge upside: But potential harms need to be managed. *The Conversation.* https://theconversation.com/artificial-intelligence-carries-a-huge-upside-but-potential-harms-need-to-be-managed-173073

Giridharadas, A. (2018). *Winners take all: The elite charade of changing the world.* Knopf.

Guihot, M., Matthew, A., & Suzor, N. (2017). Nudging robots: Innovative solutions to regulate artificial intelligence. *Vanderbilt Journal of Entertainment and Technology Law, 20*(2), 385–456. https://heinonline.org/HOL/LandingPage?handle=hein.journals/vanep20&div=16

Harvey, D. (2005). *A brief history of neoliberalism.* Oxford University Press. https://doi.org/10.1093/oso/9780199283262.001.0001

Kaput, M. (2021, November 18). *20 ways AI could transform PR and communications.* Marketing Artificial Intelligence Institute. https://www.marketingaiinstitute.com/blog/how-ai-could-transform-pr-and-communications

Kiron, D., Renieris, E., & Mills, S. (2022, April 19). Why top management should focus on responsible AI. *MIT Sloan Management Review.* https://sloanreview.mit.edu/article/why-top-management-should-focus-on-responsible-ai/

Maronitis, K. (2019). Robots and immigrants: Employment, precarisation and the art of neoliberal governance. *Angles: New Perspectives on the Anglophone World, 8,* 1–18. https://doi.org/10.4000/angles.570

Metz, C. (2022, November 23). Lawsuit takes aim at the way A.I. is built. *The New York Times.* https://www.nytimes.com/2022/11/23/technology/copilot-microsoft-ai-lawsuit.html

Perrigio, B. (2023, January 18). Exclusive: Open AI used Kenyan workers on less than $2 per hour to make ChatGPT less toxic. *Time.* https://time.com/6247678/openai-chatgpt-kenya-workers/

Roberts, P. (2014). *The impulse society.* Bloomsbury.

Roose, K. (2022a, October 21). A.I.-generated art is already transforming creative work. *The New York Times.* https://www.nytimes.com/2022/10/21/technology/ai-generated-art-jobs-dall-e-2.html

Roose, K. (2022b, October 21). A coming-out party for generative A.I., Silicon Valley's new craze. *The New York Times.* https://www.nytimes.com/2022/10/21/technology/generative-ai.html

Susskind, D., & Susskind, R. (2018). The future of the professions. *Proceedings of the American Philosophical Society, 162*(2), 125–138. https://www.jstor.org/stable/45211625

Susskind, D., & Susskind, R. (2022). *The future of the professions: How technology will transform the work of human experts* (updated ed.). Oxford University Press.

Swiatek, L., & Galloway, C. (2022). Artificial intelligence and public relations: Growing opportunities, questions, and concerns. In D. Pompper, K. R. Place, & C. Kay Weaver (Eds.), *The Routledge companion to public relations* (pp. 352–362). Routledge. https://doi.org/10.4324/9781003131700-32

Vujnovic, M., & Foster, J. (2022). *Higher education and disaster capitalism in the age of COVID-19*. Palgrave Macmillan. https://doi.org/10.1007/978-3-031-12370-2

Weitzner, D. (2022, July 19). Push for AI innovation can create dangerous products. *The Conversation*. https://theconversation.com/push-for-ai-innovation-can-create-dangerous-products-186101

Summary

This chapter has addressed the seemingly uncritical stance that strategic communicators often take towards the introduction and implementation of AI, not just in the profession, but also more broadly in society at large. Individuals and groups, the chapter has shown, are overwhelmingly faced with the adverse effects – including threats to relationships and communities – of AI continually being speedily ushered into societies by technology companies that have little or no regulatory oversight. The chapter has situated these processes within the context of expanding neoliberal global capitalism. It has also ultimately explained why communication professionals must take a more critical stance towards these developments and serve as critical voices rather than AI champions.

3   From Advocates to Activists

Strategic communicators might not yet be critical AI activists, but many of them have become concerned about AI (and related) technologies. For instance, public relations practitioners in Aotearoa New Zealand have reported that, although they are embracing emerging technologies (including AI), they feel uneasy about the transparency-related dilemmas and ethical challenges involved in the incorporation of the technologies into their practice, given the fact that the consequences of the implementation of these technologies are not yet fully known (Schutte, 2021). Considering the fact that, as noted by Curtin (in Buhmann & White, 2022, p. 625), the profession has been steadily moving from a focus on communication management towards "relationship management and social responsibility", and that it has been facing fundamental changes to practice in recent years, it is important to revisit activism in connection with public relations practitioners.

This chapter builds upon the previous chapter's content by detailing the activist role that strategic communicators can – and should – play when it comes to the implementation of AI technologies. In so doing, the chapter elaborates the book's central vision: that is, of strategic communicators becoming critical AI activists helping to counter AI-driven threats. The chapter begins by canvassing the broader need for activism in the practice of communication professionals. It then focuses more specifically on the pivot required by practitioners to shift from being organisational puppets to activists able to challenge the ill-conceived expansion of AI. After that, it discusses the importance of the activist role in relation to the need to help other publics (such as political and organisational leaders) urgently develop guardrails to protect societies from AI harms. Finally, the chapter's key points are brought together in a short conclusion.

The Broader Need for Activism in Practice

Multiple issues (not just the growth of AI) around the world that transcend individual societies behoove communication professionals to integrate activism into their practice. It is imperative that practitioners embrace activism in

DOI: 10.4324/9781003324027-3

the face of rapidly developing AI, because, as Buhmann and White (2022, p. 627) argue, many "responsibilities of AI go beyond the use of AI within the organizations in which communication professionals work". Just what kind of world we are all facing is compellingly described in the 2022 Global Communication Report, *The Future of Corporate Activism*, issued by the University of Southern California Annenberg's Center for Public Relations. The report focuses on "societal discord", as well as "continued political conflict" and the "extended global pandemic" (USC Annenberg Center for Public Relations, 2022, p. 1), to argue that our world has become more polarised and, within it, the "media has become more biased, information has become more unreliable, and opinions have become more extreme".

In addition to these identified issues, AI represents another significant change that will extensively shape the future not only of public relations, but also of communication more broadly. Indeed, information manipulation and the information wars will become even more intensive as a result of the use of AI, which will play the dual role of both curbing and spreading misinformation. Researchers have already used the generative AI tool ChatGPT to generate convincing disinformation text; they have found that, more so than not, ChatGPT "repeated conspiracy theories and misleading narratives" (Hsu & Thompson, 2023, para. 1). This example highlights the fact that organisations and strategic communication practitioners will have to be more critical, more vigilant, and more "willing to engage with controversial topics outside of their normal comfort zone"; in other words, they will have to become "socially conscious communicators, who are exploring the risks and rewards of corporate activism" (USC Annenberg Center for Public Relations, 2022, p. 3). With regard to AI, as Buhmann and White (2022, p. 627) note, communication practitioners will have to become skilled in evaluating the "moral and ethical implications of AI", and will have to learn to "balance organization policies and use of AI with the public interest".

No other issue, apart from climate change, has arguably put so much pressure on the practice to tip the scales towards working in the public interest and, specifically, in an activist capacity. The challenges stemming from AI collectively promise to unsettle (at best) and reshape (at worst) our total system of social relations. It would not be too far-fetched to say that the future of humanity, or at least the elements that define us all as humans, are being questioned and, perhaps, even threatened by the new AI craze. The world also needs to grapple with the profit-driven competition-generated Big Tech that drives AI technologies into rapid but (as discussed in the previous chapter) unfettered, unregulated and uncontrolled waters. This process is similar to the one that affected the evolution of the Internet, whose growth has been unrestrained due to both neoliberalism and the ideology of freedom of information (enabling citizens to access information without restraint). Populations around the globe are now reaping the consequences of these ideologies in the form of enormous issues with misinformation, which has led to a more polarised world. AI is already generating significant impacts, but societies' systems are still being guided by the existing ideologies. Thankfully, some positive movement is evident, particularly in Europe, in the push for digital sovereignty – "the right of a state to govern its networks to serve national interests, the most important of which are security, privacy, and economic health" (Lewis, 2020, para. 15) – that will result in stronger laws protecting the rights of citizens.

Embracing Activism

It is in this context that communication practitioners need to pivot from being AI champions to critical AI activists. These professionals, in becoming activists (Holtzhausen, 2012), should avoid seeing the technologies as being "potential equalizers" (Coombs, 1998, p. 289) that can serve as tools in helping to achieve activist goals; rather, the professionals should take a critical view of the technologies (at all times bearing in mind the manifold problems that they generate), resist the uncritical implementation of AI in organisational and societal contexts, and collectively become the voice for those who will be left behind: those who will suffer the gravest consequences and be unable to reap the benefits of AI's growth and increasing usage. The concerns relating to AI are multifold, and range from epistemic concerns that include our inability to predict AI systems' actions fully (because of the technologies' self-learning abilities) to outcome concerns that are reflected in the discrimination and bias that can be inherent in many AI systems (because of the built-in biases and discrimination inherent in the vast sets of data that AI uses); on that note, concerns about evidence are also warranted, due to the fallibility of the data that is collected and used (Buhmann & White, 2022, pp. 631–632). The critical AI activism of communication professionals does not necessarily need to be complex or all-consuming. As Galloway and Swiatek (2018, p. 736) note, there is no need for practitioners to become "expert technologists"; rather, they should acquire enough competency to offer solid advice, and to argue for organisational transparency. Buhmann and White (2022, p. 633) also observe that:

> public relations as relationship management positions communicators in a "boundary spanning" role that allows them to serve as the corporate or organizational conscience that includes securing an organization's legitimacy through aligning policies and procedures to the organization with the public interest.

Buhmann and White (2022, pp. 634–635) suggest engaging stakeholders, as well, in discourse by facilitating access to inclusive and continuous debate, facilitating comprehension, and creating opportunities for open discussion and deliberation. Although these suggestions for encouraging and facilitating debate are valuable, communication practitioners should go beyond fostering discourse and sharing knowledge about AI with stakeholders. Communicators must actively develop strategies and tactics to influence societal stakeholders outside of their organisations to act in the best interest of publics, instead of pursuing purely profit-driven motivations.

One example of such activism has been the work of the Global Strategic Communications Council (GSCC). With its partners, the GSCC has toiled to counter years of intentional public relations efforts by fossil fuel companies to push their collective point of view and manipulate information for their own profit-driven interests (Wheaton, 2021, para. 9). The activism of the GSCC – a network made up of over 100 public relations professionals in more than 20 countries – was born out of "PR trauma" caused by Big Oil's many years of using PR as a propaganda tool for climate denialism; the Council's goal was to "push a unified message from a diverse group of sources: Climate change is real, it's caused by humans, and something needs to be done about it immediately" (Wheaton, 2021, para. 4). The GSCC's major strategy was to engage stakeholders at the 2015 United Nations Climate Change Conference in Paris to help advance the perception of a united front in combatting climate action (Wheaton, 2021, para. 27). For this strategy to work, anonymity was key; as such, it is important to emphasise that, in terms of activism, public relations practitioners need to balance full transparency and secrecy in connection with incredibly consequential actions for society at large. In addition, the GSCC has actively worked on the ground, and with other stakeholders, to promote the science behind climate change and increase the sense of urgency behind the issue. Building relationships with key stakeholders – and, in particular, climate journalists – was an important strategy. A similar strategy is needed for the situation with rapidly developing AI that is facing the whole world. The new Big Oil is now Big Tech, which sanctimoniously pushes its own narratives around AI technologies as the collective solution to everyone's problems while masking profit-making incentives. To be clear, AI has multiple benefits, as do fossil fuels; however, AI, like those fuels, is now being used and advanced to the point where it is threatening the survival of the planet's life-forms (especially human beings).

Urgently Developing Guardrails

Not enough guardrails (and broader security measures) are being put in place to ensure that AI does not become more harmful than useful. Since 2015, Giddens has been calling for a Magna Carta for the digital age that, as Castinado (2018, para. 1) explains, would help to "reduce AI risks and guarantee the protection of individual rights while also fostering innovation in technology"; this idea draws on the 1215 charter that King John of England signed that "outlin[es] individuals' basic rights and the foundational social contracts between ruler and subject that underlay modern governments" (Castinado, 2018, para. 3). Lord Giddens and 13 other members of the UK's House of Lords Select Committee on Artificial Intelligence, after interviewing a diverse group of over 60 AI experts, issued a report separating the hype from the real dangers surrounding digital transformations. In its report, the committee warns that, just as with the first and second iterations of the Internet, the AI-powered third age of the Internet is a potential threat to the liberties that were guaranteed by the Magna Carta: liberties that are inherent in constitutions in most Western democracies. Giddens (in Castinado, 2018, para. 5) has remarked that:

> For a while, the positive breakthroughs of digital technologies – greater connectivity among like-minded peers or distant scholars, big data analysis of the genetic code, the convenience of online shopping – took center stage. But the negative aspects have proven to be profound, even though they took time to surface. They include threats to the very tissue of democracy itself – online movements have come to challenge or even displace mainstream political parties. These are emerging at the same time as what look like dramatic advances in machine learning.

The varying but rapid speeds at which these advances are taking place, as well as the negative impacts that they are generating, mean that guardrails need to be created swiftly.

The profound and wide-ranging influences of emerging technologies on our political, social, cultural and economic relations merit at least a healthy dose of skepticism on the part of strategic communicators (and, frankly, all of us), especially in relation to cheerleading or advocacy for the technologies. It is incumbent upon communication professionals to play less of a facilitating role and more of an activist role in warning of the real dangers that under-regulated AI (in the context of laissez-faire capitalism, in particular) poses to societies at large and, potentially (much like climate change), to human existence. This position is logical, rather than alarmist; following deductive reasoning, a significant amount of evidence has already accumulated that shows the adverse effects of leaving emerging technologies in the hands of business ventures without proper restrictions. While our democratic institutions have established social contracts between the constituent and the government, similar contracts have not been drawn up between the stakeholder and the organisation (especially the corporation). While some companies are moving, at least on paper, towards ensuring greater responsibility not only for their immediate stakeholders, but also for society at large, Big Tech is actively applying pressure to government using the old lobbying playbook; for instance, it is fighting antitrust laws, using multimillion-dollar campaigns that urge lawmakers to leave technology alone and not to break things that, in its view, work (Wheeler, 2022).

Conclusion

Given the mounting problems, at both the micro and macro levels, being generated by AI, the need for strategic communicators to shift from being advocates to activists has never been greater. As Buhmann and White (2022, p. 636) comment, the practitioners need "to develop a greater level of critical literacy and understanding about the use and societal impacts of AI"; this professional growth is especially important given the fact that research has already found that "professional communicators may currently be buying into process they do not fully understand". There is certainly a sense of urgency surrounding the need for these shifts, as many different kinds of canaries have been whistling in various coal mines (as this chapter has outlined) about AI issues; as such, it is more important than ever for communicators to act swiftly and create relationships with other societal stakeholders, such as experts and media professionals, to increase AI risk awareness and help to protect organisations, groups and individuals, especially those who are already on the margins of society. The next chapter outlines the theoretical and practical approaches that communication professionals can use to undertake their critical AI activist work.

References

Buhmann, A., & White, C. L. (2022). Artificial intelligence in public relations: Role and implications. In J. H. Lipschultz, K. Freberg, & R. Luttrell (Eds.), *The Emerald handbook of computer-mediated communication and social media* (pp. 625–638). Emerald. https://doi.org/10.1108/978-1-80071-597-420221036

Castinado, J. (2018, May 7). UK Lord: AI developers urgently need 21st century guidelines. *Seeflection.* https://seeflection.com/16034/ai-development-in-urgent-need-of-21st-century-guidelines/

Coombs, W. T. (1998). The Internet as potential equalizer: New leverage for confronting social irresponsibility. *Public Relations Review, 24*(3), 289–303. https://doi.org/10.1016/S0363-8111(99)80141-6

Galloway, C., & Swiatek, L. (2018). Public relations and artificial intelligence: It's not (just) about robots. *Public Relations Review, 44*(5), 734–740. https://doi.org/10.1016/j.pubrev.2018.10.008

Holtzhausen, D. R. (2012). *Public relations as activism: Postmodern approaches to theory & practice.* Routledge. https://doi.org/10.4324/9780203819098

Hsu, T., & Thompson, S. A. (2023, February 8). Disinformation researchers raise alarms about A.I. chatbots. *The New York Times.* https://www.nytimes.com/2023/02/08/technology/ai-chatbots-disinformation.html

Lewis, J. A. (2020, October 30). *Sovereignty and the evolution of Internet ideology.* Center for Strategic and International Studies. https://www.csis.org/analysis/sovereignty-and-evolution-internet-ideology

Schutte, K. (2021). *Emerging technologies: Perspectives of New Zealand public relations practitioners* [Doctoral thesis, Auckland University of Technology]. http://orapp.aut.ac.nz/handle/10292/13963

USC Annenberg Center for Public Relations. (2022). *The future of corporate activism.* 2022 Global Communication Report. https://issuu.com/uscannenberg/docs/usc_cpr_global_communication_report_2022

Wheaton, S. (2021, November 9). The climate activists stealing Big Oil's playbook. *Politico.* https://www.politico.eu/article/the-climate-activists-stealing-big-oils-playbook/

Wheeler, T. (2022, June 15). History repeats itself with Big Tech's misleading advertising. *TechTank (Brookings Institute).* https://www.brookings.edu/blog/techtank/2022/06/15/history-repeats-itself-with-big-techs-misleading-advertising/

Summary

This chapter has expatiated the book's central vision: of strategic communicators becoming critical AI activists (instead of being advocates for AI). The adverse impacts on human relationships and society at large generated by AI necessitate this shift on the part of communication professionals. The chapter has outlined the broader need for activism, detailed the pivot required by practitioners, and considered the importance of the activist role in terms of the urgent need to help other publics (especially lawmakers and policy experts) develop guardrails to protect societies from the ever-increasing harms brought about by the use of AI. In the coming years, as this chapter has discussed, the need will grow for communicators to raise publics' awareness of the dangers of the unrestrained, profit-driven Big Tech push for AI expansion, and to work with multiple stakeholders (such as media professionals and experts) to help protect individuals, groups and organisations, as well as human relationships and communities.

4   Theory and Practice to Support Activism

The context for communication professionals' activism must begin with the consideration of a meta-question that was often posed by Carey, the preeminent communication scholar, who would ask his students: "How is society possible?" Carey's answer was abstracted and interpreted by Pauly (1997, pp. 3–4) thus:

> [S]ociety is possible only in and through communication. Our symbolic acts call society into existence and sustain its presence among us, making our relations amenable, investing the world with significance, offering us shared models of identity, tutoring us in common modes of interpretation.

Hardt (1979) additionally emphasised that that such examination must begin within the context of a theory of society that defines the position of that society's individual members, thus emphasising the particular (and not just the universal). In light of society's constitution through communication, the ideal professionals to help defend society against AI threats are strategic communicators, who not only have a deep understanding of the importance of communication and the crucialness of relationships, but are also able to use their communication skills and knowledge to effect positive change in multiple (micro- and macro-level) contexts. To effect this sort of change, these professionals must play a more activist role, as this book argues, in their organisations and communities.

This chapter outlines the approaches – both theoretical and practical – that these professionals can use to undertake critical AI activism. It builds on the previous chapter, and its discussion of the pivot from pro-AI advocacy to counter-AI activism, by providing a toolbox of sorts that professionals can use in their work. As practitioners' critical AI activities gain momentum, they can (and should) expand the number and types of tasks that they undertake. Specifically, they should: assume increasing responsibility for assessing the ethical ramifications of their organisations' applications of specific AI technologies; help, as needed, to defend organisations, groups and communities from AI threats; and play a growing part in organisational leadership to identify

DOI: 10.4324/9781003324027-4

and neutralise AI developments that are deleterious to internal and external publics. The chapter begins by explaining in greater detail why communication professionals are so well placed to counter AI-driven threats. It then outlines theoretical tools that can support communicator-activists, after which it canvasses practical tools that can aid the activists. Next, it discusses broader considerations that strategic communicators need to keep in mind in their activism. A short conclusion brings the chapter to a close.

Strategic Communicators' Suitability for Critical AI Activism

Thanks to their awareness of the importance of human relationships, their relationship-building skills, and their long-proven ability to develop and disseminate compelling messages, strategic communicators are well placed to counter AI threats to groups, organisations and broader communities. One of the professionals' particularly salient communication competencies is their "translation of technical information to readily understandable messaging"; this strength enables them to be in a position to explicate AI developments and the problems connected to them effectively and efficiently, in both public and private settings (Swiatek et al., 2022, p. 657). A communicator's wider skillset is also invaluable for activist work. The practitioner – who, by virtue of the profession and the training (as well as ongoing professional development) that it provides, successfully "shapes meaning, builds trust, creates reputation, and manages symbolic relationships with internal and external stakeholders" (Zerfass & Huck, 2007, p. 108) – is well placed to undertake the interpersonal, group, organisational and public communication-related activities that activism requires. Additionally, these professionals' generally close proximity to the C-suite (that is, to the organisation's leadership team) means that they can provide effective 'second-order management' and successfully liaise with executives in a "soft, influential and diplomatic way" (Frandsen & Johansen, 2014, p. 240) in furthering all kinds of activist initiatives, both large and small.

The pivot of communication professionals towards activism is in line with the changing nature of the communication profession itself. Kruckeberg (2022) has observed that the profession is both temporal and dynamic; its mission, values, ethics, and best practices must be continually re-examined within the context of society's constantly changing social, political, economic, and cultural dimensions. Appropriate responses to these changes, he notes, might result in the demise of the profession's present 'life cycle'. As Darwin would contend, a new life cycle for a species might introduce a better-adapted mutation of that species (instead of signalling its extinction). Future junctures in the profession's present life cycle might result in significant deviations in its practice, scholarship, and education to address contemporary and future challenges more effectively. These transformations are needed given the fact that today's media landscape "is replete with the ubiquitous use of artificial intelligence and of fake news, lies, misinformation, disinformation, ambiguous sources and a host of other variables that confound and are highly threatening to the integrity of communication" (Kruckeberg, 2023, paras. 15–16). Nearly three decades ago, Kruckeberg (1996) already predicted that public relations practitioners – if they proved themselves worthy of the task – would be called upon to be organisational interpreters, ethicists and social policy-makers, charged with guiding organisational behaviour, as well as with influencing and reconciling public perceptions within a global context.

In the new life cycle of public relations, professional practice will involve activism much more extensively, in light of the general global shift towards activism, the growing importance of organisational social responsibility and the worldwide expansion of social movements (discussed in the previous chapter). In terms of AI, communication professionals' future responsibilities should increase, enabling them to: become progressively more and more responsible for assessing the ethical ramifications of their organisations' applications of AI; help, where necessary, to defend groups, organisations and communities from AI threats; and play an ever-larger role in organisational leadership to neutralise AI developments that are harmful to internal and external publics of various kinds. These activities clearly align with the mission, role and function of organisations' public relations practitioners; however, a reorientation towards a worldview of activism is required. To become successful practitioner-activists, communication professionals will need to have a prerequisite understanding of, and a continuing commitment to embracing, the activist role; they will need to adapt, refine, and build upon the growing body of knowledge and best practices of activism. Such a reorientation and worldview ultimately support organisations, which benefit from – and, indeed, need – practitioner-activists. The role of the organisational ethicist is consistent within this reorientation. As Rubin (1978) has correctly observed, no ethical standards are built into the mass media. This certainly holds true in today's digital multimedia environment. Thus, it is important for the public relations practitioner to act as an "ombudsman" who can advocate and fight for both organisational and (external) publics' interests (Vujnovic, 2004). This view echoes Holtzhausen and Voto's (2002) argument that public relations practitioners can serve as organisational advocates for the concerns that are voiced by external publics.

Theory to Support Activism

An understanding of several concepts related to communication is essential for professionals to undertake critical AI activism. The professionals will likely already be familiar with these concepts in connection with their existing roles within their organisations. The first of these concepts (as outlined by Vujnovic & Kruckeberg, 2016, p. 124) is authenticity: the attributes of a social actor that are truthfully presented not only to that social actor's publics and to society at large, but also to the actor (in having knowledge of who or what the actors is). (This concept will help professionals to remember to distinguish between AI and AI-developed content, ranging from text to deepfakes, and humans and human-developed content.) Understanding pseudotransparency is also crucial for the critical AI activist work of communicators; this concept refers to a false sense of both voluntarily and involuntarily disclosed, easily accessible, shared information, which, through the means of new communication technologies, is usually immediate and inexpensive, if not free. (This concept will likely especially help communicators to approach the claims, and particularly the information disclosures, of Big Tech critically.) Another key concept for practitioners to bear in mind throughout their activities is transparency, which arises when information is shared – both voluntarily and involuntarily – in addition to being easily accessible and, thanks to new communication technologies, usually immediate and inexpensive, if not free. (Communicators will do well to make information about AI, and especially organisations' AI activities, transparent.) The concept of trust is also vital, and refers to a confident belief in the authenticity of a social actor. (Communicators should keep in mind that publics will only have faith in organisations, groups and communities when they trust that AI is being used properly.)

Several additional concepts should also be borne in mind by communication professionals. These concepts (outlined by Tsetsura & Kruckeberg, 2017) will help the professionals to ensure that they challenge the harms arising from deleterious AI use and, at the same time, operate in ways that strengthen organisations, groups, communities and individual relationships. Communicators should always remember – and operate in ways that ensure – truth, which can be viewed as accurate, unbiased and complete information that has been gathered and verified competently and conscientiously, and that is presented fairly and in good faith by those who are attempting to achieve the ideal of objectivity with complete transparency in gathering, analysing, and presenting the information. (Communicators will need to ensure that they communicate truthfully about AI, the problems that it generates, and the ways in which organisations make use of AI.) At all times, professionals should avoid lying: that is, delivering information known to be false and presenting it with the intent to deceive or mislead. (Needless to say, lying about AI and the issues that it entails should be avoided because of the damage that lying causes to relationships, reputations and trust, among other things.) Communicators should also avoid providing any sort of incomplete truth, which refers to information being accurate by and large, but having contextualising information intentionally omitted or influences not disclosed, as a result altering the presentation of the information, with an outcome of deceiving and/or misleading. (The communication of incomplete truths about AI would similarly result in all manner of damage.) When professionals engage in persuasive communication activities, especially for the sake of critical AI activism, they need to remember to be transparent in their motives, ensure that no hidden influences exist, enable those receiving messages to identify their role and recognise their motives, as well as provide unlimited opportunities for recipients to respond freely to the messages (Tsetsura & Kruckeberg, 2017).

Strategic communicators should also implement ethics theories into their activist work. The classic ethics schools or approaches – deontology (adhering to rules, especially laws), virtue (aiming to be upright or having integrity as individuals) and consequentialism (actively considering the outcomes of actions) – should always be observed in all activities (Tilley, 2012). Beyond these classic approaches, other considerations relating to ethics – explored more fully in the next chapter – should be taken into account by professionals. The host of ethical questions and concerns regarding social actors' use and potential misuse of AI should always be explored and debated with colleagues (and other stakeholders and stake-seekers). Certainly, the very development and implementation of AI applications beg questions regarding truth, incomplete truth and lying, not to mention transparency and pseudotransparency, as well as authenticity and trust. Even base assumptions concerning human agency – for example, whether a person is engaging in dialogue with a human or with a chatbot – should be scrutinised and discussed as widely as possible (thus also furthering activist work). In that respect, the practitioner should aim to gather and consider both professional and extra-professional insights. Indeed, as Olen (1988) has noted, professional ethics are shaped by two distinct forces: (1) the wider moral principles of a society; and (2) the aims of the occupation; society's general moral principles ultimately provide overall constraints on these aims and on the ways in which professional functions may be executed. On this broader level, society at large needs to consider more fully, and with quite some urgency, the ethical ramifications of AI more extensively; communication practitioner-activists, through their use and discussion of ethics, can contribute to that fuller consideration of these ramifications.

Practice to Support Activism

Communication professionals can make use of a wide range of activist techniques or approaches to challenge the expansion, implementation and celebration of AI, beginning with small-scale, everyday actions. These types of actions have been labelled 'quiet activism' and refer to "intimate and embodied acts of collective disruption, subversion, creativity and care at the local scale" (Steele et al., 2021, p. 2). Distinct from "vocal and antagonistic forms of protest", quiet activism focuses on local, socially engaged and often informal activities; this type of activism emphasises "the power of small, purposeful everyday practices of resistance and rebellion, the politics of making and doing, and the ways in which this produces both the means and conditions through which alternative values can be explored and shared" (Steele et al., 2021, p. 2). In terms of professional communicators' counter-AI efforts, quiet activism can usefully help practitioners, for example, to develop connections with influential stakeholders and stake-seekers who take a critical view of AI, collect stories of the damage that AI has already caused (especially in local, workplace contexts), build repositories to enable the public sharing of those stories, and help colleagues develop their skills in identifying and countering AI threats as a way of enhancing individuals' "response-ability" to new disruptions (Steele et al., 2021, p. 43).

A variety of less-quiet workplace activism approaches is also available to communication practitioners. Drawing on the now-classic typology elaborated by Scully and Segal (2002), professionals can employ familiar techniques from organisational contexts, such as holding meetings to discuss ways to counter AI harms, shape agendas to feature critical AI items (such as discussions or announcements about AI-generated problems), form subcommittees and caucus groups to investigate AI issues and coordinate action to address them, and use tools such as flip charts, email and listservs (among other types of communication collateral) for critical AI awareness-raising and action-encouragement. They can also reshape the framing of AI in workplaces and change public and private scripts by, for instance, alerting colleagues (both superiors and subordinates) to the fact that countering AI harms is good for business, and that protecting individuals can help to ensure civil rights. In order to strengthen the numbers of like-minded collaborators and build momentum for change, they can also recruit individuals using even simple approaches such as lunchtime gatherings. All of these sorts of techniques, Scully and Segal (2002, p. 140) note, are so useful because, quite simply: "Employees know how to work nimbly from inside."

Much more vocal and radical activism approaches can also be used by professional communicators, though they entail greater risks of various kinds. The professionals (drawing on Joyce, 2016) can help to mobilise employees to protest organisations' uses of AI, lead withdrawals of labour (that, most commonly, take the form of strikes), help to organise picketing and cyber-picketing in order to persuade colleagues to join strikes, and coordinate or co-coordinate 'blacking' in refusing to handle goods that feature AI connected in any way to the organisation. However, these sorts of approaches carry risks of retaliatory action by organisations (such as punishment, the concealing of AI activities, and the implementation of restrictions on employee actions), the potential use of the law to curb or end activities such as protests and strikes, the souring of relationships and the chilling of communication climates within organisations, and reputational damage (not just to organisations, but also to employees themselves, including to communication professionals). For this reason, communicators should be reluctant to make use of these more antagonistic activism approaches, or even avoid them altogether, and opt instead for the nimbler and quieter activism techniques outlined earlier in this section.

Additional Considerations for Strategic Communicator-activists

In undertaking their critical AI activist efforts, communicators need to keep in mind a number of broader considerations, with one of the most important being the nature of operating in today's complex global society. It is useless – indeed, meaningless and grossly misleading – to assume that AI can be over-layed onto a static and stable world. Vujnovic and Kruckeberg (2015) point to considerable evidence suggesting that global society is in the midst of a revolution that is fundamentally changing us all as humans. These authors observe that the changes are being caused by advances in communication technology. The authors argue that one indicator of this revolution is an individual's inability to ignore it. Save for a cataclysmic event, there is no going back to the previous circumstances. Kruckeberg (2000, pp. 152–153) had noted nearly a quarter century ago that:

> Castigating globalism and modern communication technology, and seeking regress to a pastoral and isolationist existence, can be likened to a Canutian attempt to hold back the tides. There can be no return to a pre-global and pretechnological society, nor is there a desire to do so by most people who are quick to embrace the advantages of contemporary life – despite its accompanying social problems and troubling issues of power differentials.

AI is creating new social problems and exacerbating power differentials; communication professionals need to be aware of these challenges as they go about their work.

They also need to be aware of the ongoing and significant disruptions that they will continue to see around them. Schwab (2016, p. 9) echoes the conclusions of many other scholars when he states: "Simply put, major technological innovations are on the brink of fueling momentous change throughout the world – inevitably so." Kruckeberg (2022) foresees a continuing barrage of disruptors, some that may be predictable, controllable, and that will be deemed desirable; however, other disruptors will be unpredicted, will prove deleterious, and may be revolutionary in their impact. Furthermore, Kruckeberg et al. (2014) note that control and authority are being challenged and threatened in previously unimaginable ways, including by those beyond the increasingly porous borders of nation-states. Tsetsura and Kruckeberg (2019) have warned that "we are sailing in uncharted waters that likely will have unpredicted and unintended consequences". Indeed, Vujnovic and Kruckeberg (2012) had pondered some time ago:

> whether communication technology will a) help to assure sustainable and universally prosperous lives in an equally sustainable world . . . or b) whether communication technology is a beguiling opiate of bread-and-circuses for privileged self-entitled consumers playing "angry birds," i.e., a narcotic that presages the demise of a sustainable civilization worldwide.

Other international forces, especially rising geopolitical tensions (not to mention large-scale conflicts in some parts of the world), are contributing to the weakening of sustainable civilisation at present.

Additional, longstanding problems will continue to confront communication professionals and make their activist work more challenging. The existing problems include massive migrations of the world's population, creating global instability, and the immense numbers of individuals worldwide who have little or no education and little promise of future personal sustainability (Tsetsura & Kruckeberg, 2019). Will the world be sustainable in the next decade, socially, politically, economically, and culturally, as well as environmentally? It is no exaggeration to suggest that global society may be at a critical juncture. Tsetsura and Kruckeberg (2019) are among those who argue that today's paradigms of global society must be re-examined. Importantly, they emphasise that such paradigmatic re-examination should not imply that new paradigms necessarily will be ethically and morally superior to the ones that they have replaced.

It is within this context of today's unstable and rapidly changing global society and tomorrow's uncertain – indeed, largely unknown – world in which AI must be considered. It is especially important for strategic communicators to remember that AI is amorphous, remains ill-defined, and is unpredictable in its continuing evolution. It is likely that AI will continue to generate unintended consequences for all sorts of social actors. For these reasons, 1,000 AI experts and technology industry leaders have called for a six-month pause in the development of AI systems; in an open letter, these individuals (in Rudnitsky & Bergen, 2023, para. 4) have stated that: "Powerful AI systems should be developed only once we are confident that their effects will be positive and their risks will be manageable." Grimmelmann (in O'Brien, 2023, para. 11), though, has highlighted the issue with a simple "pause" in the development of AI, stating that: "A pause is a good idea, but . . . doesn't take the regulatory problems seriously." Chapters two and three of this book have already discussed the seriousness of the regulatory problems that negatively impact not only individuals and organisations, but also whole democracies and societies. In pondering the implications of these sorts of developments for today's global society, Kruckeberg (2000, p. 146) had noted some time ago that "massive technological changes – evolving within an extraordinarily short time frame – have tremendous and little understood implications for society and heretofore unmeasured impact on individuals". These implications and impacts make the activist work of communication practitioners all the more important, in spite of the speedbumps that the professionals will encounter along the way.

Conclusion

A variety of theoretical and practical tools is available to help strategic communicators succeed in their critical AI activism efforts, and this chapter has outlined the most significant of those tools. In so doing, it has also explained why communicators are the ideal professionals to undertake this activism work. This explanation aligns with Vujnovic's (2004) queries about the public relations practitioner being part of an organisation's dominant coalition, because organisational loyalty hinders the ability of the practitioner to serve as a dissenting voice within the organisation. This chapter, in charting the ways in which the practitioner can undertake dissenting work relating to AI, has also outlined the additional, broader considerations that professionals need to take into account in their activist efforts. The next chapter, as noted previously, discusses ethics-related issues in greater detail.

References

Frandsen, F., & Johansen, W. (2014). The role of communication executives in strategy and strategizing. In D. Holtzhausen & A. Zerfass (Eds.), *The Routledge handbook of strategic communication* (pp. 229–243). Routledge. https://doi.org/10.4324/9780203094440-23

Hardt, H. (1979). *Social theories of the press*. Sage.

Holtzhausen, D. R., & Voto, R. (2002). Resistance from the margins: The postmodern public relations practitioner as organizational activist. *Journal of Public Relations Research, 14*(1), 57–84. https://doi.org/10.1207/S1532754XJPRR1401_3

Joyce, P. (2016). *The policing of protest, disorder and international terrorism in the UK since 1945*. Palgrave Macmillan. https://doi.org/10.1057/978-1-137-29059-5

Kruckeberg, D. (1996, Winter). The challenges for public relations in the era of globalization. *Public Relations Quarterly, 40*(4), 36–39.

Kruckeberg, D. (2000). Public relations: Toward a global professionalism. In J. A. Ledingham & S. D. Bruning (Eds.), *Public relations as relationship management: A relational approach to the study and practice of public relations* (pp. 145–157). Lawrence Erlbaum.

Kruckeberg, D. (2022). Foreword. In D. Pompper, K. R. Place, & C. K. Weaver (Eds.), *The Routledge companion to public relations* (pp. xii–xvii). Routledge. https://doi.org/10.4324/9781003131700

Kruckeberg, D. (2023, January 9). International thought leader # 506: Sailing in uncharted waters: Communications in an era of massive and insufficiently understood changes. *IPRA*. https://www.ipra.org/news/itle/itl-506-sailing-in-uncharted-waters-communications-in-an-era-of-massive-and-insufficiently-understood-changes/

Kruckeberg, D., Creedon, P., Gorpe, S., & Al-Khajha, M. (2014, October). *The dynamics of power and influence among corporations, civil society organizations and governments: Ramifications of the changing social, political, economic and cultural dimensions of global society in an era of transparency through digital communication.* Paper presented at the 19th Annual Conference of the Arab-U.S. Association for Communication Educators, Irbid, Jordan.

O'Brien, M. (2023, March 30). Musk, scientists call for halt to AI race sparked by ChatGPT. *ABC News.* https://abcnews.go.com/Business/wireStory/musk-scientists-call-halt-ai-race-sparked-chatgpt-98208068

Olen, J. (1988). *Ethics in journalism.* Prentice Hall.

Pauly, J. (1997). Introduction/on the origins of media studies (and media scholars). In E. S. Munson & C. A. Warren (Eds.), *James Carey: A critical reader* (pp. 3–13). The University of Minnesota Press.

Rubin, B. (1978). The search for media ethics. In B. Rubin (Ed.), *Questioning media ethics.* Praeger.

Rudnitsky, J., & Bergen, M. (2023, March 30). Musk, Wozniak urge halt to more powerful AI models. *Financial Review.* https://www.afr.com/technology/musk-wozniak-call-for-halt-on-developing-more-powerful-ai-models-20230330-p5cwhs

Schwab, K. (2016). *The fourth industrial revolution.* Crown Business.

Scully, M., & Segal, A. (2002). Passion with an umbrella: Grassroots activists in the workplace. In M. Lounsbury & M. J. Ventresca (Eds.), *Social structure and organizations revisited* (pp. 125–168). Emerald. https://doi.org/10.1016/S0733-558X(02)19004-5

Steele, W., Hillier, J., MacCallum, D., Byrne, J., & Houston, D. (2021). *Quiet activism: Climate action at the local scale.* Palgrave Macmillan. https://doi.org/10.1007/978-3-030-78727-1

Swiatek, L., Galloway, C., Vujnovic, M., & Kruckeberg, D. (2022). Artificial intelligence and changing ethical landscapes in social media and computer-mediated communication: Considering the role of communication professionals. In J. H. Lipschultz, K. Freberg, & R. Luttrell (Eds.), *The Emerald handbook of computer-mediated communication and social media* (pp. 653–670). Emerald. https://doi.org/10.1108/978-1-80071-597-420221038

Tilley, E. (2012). Public relations ethics. In J. Chia & G. Synnott (Eds.), *An introduction to public relations and communication management* (2nd ed., pp. 88–120). Oxford University Press.

Tsetsura, K., & Kruckeberg, D. (2017). *Transparency, public relations and the mass media: Combating media bribery worldwide.* Routledge. https://doi.org/10.4324/9780203545461

Tsetsura, K., & Kruckeberg, D. (2019, July). *The changing nature of journalism: A sociology of de-professionalization.* Paper presented at the 5th World Journalism Education Conference, Paris, France.

Vujnovic, M. (2004). *The public relations practitioner as ombudsman – a reconstructed model* [Unpublished master's thesis, University of Northern Iowa].

Vujnovic, M., & Kruckeberg, D. (2012, March). *Public relations and community: A reconstructed theory revisited (once again).* Paper presented at the 15th annual International Public Relations Research Conference, Miami, FL.

Vujnovic, M., & Kruckeberg, D. (2015). Conceptualization, examination, and recommendations for a normative model of community-building for organizations managing change using new media. In E.-J. Ki, J.-N. Kim, & J. Ledingham (Eds.), *Public* relations as relationship management: A relational approach to the study and practice of public relations (2nd ed.). Routledge. https://doi.org/10.4324/9781315719559-19

Vujnovic, M., & Kruckeberg, D. (2016). Pitfalls and promises of transparency in the digital age. *Public Relations Inquiry, 5*(2), 121–143. https://doi.org/10.1177/2046147X16635227

Zerfass, A., & Huck, S. (2007). Innovation, communication, and leadership: New developments in strategic communication. *International Journal of Strategic Communication, 1*(2), 107–122. https://doi.org/10.1080/15531180701298908

Summary

This chapter has outlined the rich theoretical and applied approaches that communication professionals can use to undertake critical AI activist work. It has noted that the number and types of tasks that practitioners undertake can (and should) expand as their activist efforts gain momentum. These practitioners – who are the ideal professionals to undertake these efforts due to their understanding of the importance of (human) relationships, their skills in relationship-building, and their ability to develop and deliver compelling messages – should actively build their activist knowledge and hone their skills. The chapter has also discussed the broader, international issues that the communicators need to consider in undertaking activist work.

5 Beyond Reactive Ethics

In both the long and short terms, strategic communicators will not only need to integrate ethics actively into their critical AI activism, but also increasingly take a more intentional rather than reactive approach to ethics. The domains of AI communication ethics and, more broadly, AI ethics are issues-rich, debate-heavy domains dominated by discussions of the ethical implications of emerging technologies as they arrive. A prime example is ChatGPT, released in November 2022, and its accelerating ability to produce plausible, if often superficial and even inaccurate, text. Groll (2023, para. 1) contends, in terms of international relations, that such tools "are poised to transform how nations deploy digital propaganda operations to manipulate public opinion". In education, fears have mounted of "a tsunami of cheating" (Rowan in Miles, 2023, para. 27). Communicators should not be exempt from confronting AI developments' built-in ethical problems, captured neatly in the headline: "When algorithms rule, values can wither" (Lindebaum et al., 2022). The challenge is significant; as Heilinger (2022, p. 61) notes, "the term AI itself can give rise to misleading intuitions, which may subsequently influence AI ethics itself by creating an idea of the technology . . . that does not match with its reality". Even those involved in designing and implementing AI applications cannot necessarily predict a system's behavior (Kinderlerer in Stahl, 2021, p. v).

This chapter discusses the ethical challenges connected to critical AI activism (as well as AI more generally, especially in relation to communication), and explores the ways in which communication professionals can take intentional, rather than reactive, approaches to ethics. Following Leslie (2019), AI ethics is understood, here, as "a set of values, principles, and techniques that employ widely accepted standards of right and wrong to guide moral conduct in the development and use of AI technologies". Already, AI ethics is an extensive, fast-growing and discrete research area that, nevertheless, is "still in the infancy stage", according to Siau and Wang (2020, p. 74). Arguably, the area offers more questions than answers; Stahl (2021, p. 2) suggests that, while the assertion that AI raises ethical concerns is largely uncontentious, "[w]hat is less clear is what exactly constitutes the ethical concerns, why they are of an ethical nature, who should address them and how they are to be dealt

DOI: 10.4324/9781003324027-5

with". The chapter first discusses the unpredictable environments in which communicators must face AI-related ethical questions. It then examines ethics and regulatory interventions, especially ethics guidelines or 'charters' and their limits. Next, it explores the challenge of trust in relation to AI and ethics, focusing on AI biases. After that, it outlines a novel approach, making use of the Global Alliance for Public Relations and Communication Management, to facilitate collaboration among communication professionals to tackle AI ethics issues. In outlining this approach, it challenges the professionals to engage with fraught issues such as regulation and governance. The chapter's points are brought to a close through a short conclusion.

Unpredictable Contexts for Ethical Questions

The unpredictability of the broad environments in which strategic communicators will continually be required to deal with AI ethics challenges cannot be overstated. Given the ongoing and significant shifts in these environments, no professional can claim 'completeness' (see Heilinger, 2022, p. 61); rather, practitioners can attempt to identify key issues and propose approaches to them, including assuming an individual responsibility to keep abreast of major developments. Addressing communicators, Graham (2023, para. 13) notes that: "As AI evolves so do the ethical issues it raises. We need to be fully cognisant of future developments and get our heads round the likely consequences." For example, Borremans (2023, para. 4) notes that ChatGPT is currently unable to understand emotions behind text, and has difficulty with open-ended questions. Such issues – even though they may be dealt with in updated versions of the tools – typify a technological and ethical landscape shot through with uncertainty. As Kruckeberg (2023, para. 16) argues, "communication technology has created an unpredictable and threatening global environment in which massive and insufficiently understood changes are occurring".

With so much uncertainty to navigate, momentous challenges lie ahead. As AI ethics debates continue, many commentators address communication and the issues surrounding it only implicitly rather than explicitly. The result is a lacuna that leaves would-be principled communicators plenty of room to form their own conclusions. It is in this environment of "radical uncertainty" (Kay & King, 2020) that, frequently, pressing ethical issues must be faced: issues intrinsic not just to AI and its impacts (short- and long-term), but also to communication itself. Kazim and Hilliard (2022, p. 6) argue that, while one can point out moral harms, "in the majority of cases ethical clarity is not available and . . . debate/nuance is needed . . . to come to a mature and rational position". Despite this murkiness, questions about ethics abound. As Lipari (2017, para. 2) remarks:

> both communication and ethics are tacitly or explicitly inherent in all
> human interactions, [and] everyday life is fraught with intentional and

unintentional ethical questions – from reaching for a cup of coffee to speaking up in a public meeting. Thus, ethical questions infuse all areas of the discipline of communication.

Those questions (including ones about coffee) are worked out either by intent or by default, whether the intent is that of a group of AI developers or of a machine's self-learning.

Communication practitioners thus need to keep in mind the sources of different perspectives about, and approaches to, ethics. In this respect, Kantrowitz (2023, para. 5) aptly observes that "AI's intelligence may be artificial, but humans encode its values". Of course, coding for an AI system is a pre-implementation activity; often, however, communication ethics are an ex post facto consideration. That is, a communicator decides to compose something (such as a piece of text) and, having made that decision, thinks about whether the content will meet ethical guidelines (if the communicator in question considers those guidelines at all). Despite authors such as Baker and Martinson (2001) advocating "ethically proactive public relations", and Siau and Wang (2020, p. 84) asserting that "AI ethics should be the central consideration in developing AI agents and not an afterthought", ethics may still come to the fore only in retrospect, when it becomes clear that some communication or other development has breached ethical norms and the potential consequences of that breach must be confronted.

Reactive approaches to ethics still seem to be the norm not only in communication in general, but also – and arguably, especially – in digital communication. As Meng et al. (2022, p. 581) note, "there is a wide range of ethical challenges in digital [professional communication] practices". Kane (2019, para. 6) also remarks that "[d]igital ethics can often seem like a part that's bolted on after the corporate engine has been built and tuned", notwithstanding the availability of digital ethics guidelines, such as those developed by the Austrian Public Relations Ethics Council (2017) and recommended by institutions such as the International Communications Consultancy Organisation. Most ethics-related controversies refer to decisions already made. As such, it is worth asking: what about choices yet to take shape, such as the creation of new algorithms for communication purposes, whether to inform, promote or propagandise? In the academic arena, Stanford University now requires AI researchers to evaluate their proposals for any potential negative impacts on society *before* funding for those proposals can be obtained from the Stanford Institute for Human-Centered Artificial Intelligence (Jensen, 2021). Yet, outside college walls, the issue of how to assess the ethics of planned AI implementations is complicated by the fact that "AI developers often lack sufficient expertise to understand potential abuses of the technologies they create" (Goldstein et al., 2023, p. 64). Therefore, the developers may be unreliable guides with respect to possible ethical issues.

Ethics and Regulatory Interventions

In the face of the multiple dilemmas confronting communication professionals, questions of external regulatory interventions arise. The UK Government,
for instance, operates a pro-innovation strategy that focuses on regulating
the *use* of AI, not the technology itself. The government recognises that "AI
often demonstrates a high degree of autonomy, operating in dynamic and
fast-moving environments by automating complex cognitive tasks" (UK
Government, 2022, para. 39). This assessment highlights the challenge of
developing, sharing and (if need be) actively guiding on ethical paths those
who build, advocate for, and use AI technologies. The UK Government
(2022, para. 47) also notes that "AI technologies feature a range of underlying issues and risks which require a coherent response, such as a perceived
lack of explainability when high-impact decisions are made about people
using AI". Yet, the very dynamism to which the government refers works
against the coherence being sought; it is as if goalposts were forever shift-
ing. Therefore, the UK Government envisages implementing a set of cross-
sectoral principles that amount to aspirational goals freighted with *ante
facto* communication requirements, not to mention ethical assumptions. Its
proposals (as of January 2023) are to:

- ensure that AI is used safely,
- make certain that AI is technically secure and functions as designed,
- confirm that AI is appropriately transparent and explainable,
- embed considerations of fairness into AI,
- define legal persons' responsibility for AI governance, and
- clarify routes to redress or contestability.

As AI evolves, these proposals will likely need to be revised and expanded.
The ethical assumptions underlying the proposals may also need to be
revisited.

In recent years, the number of dedicated government institutions tackling
AI ethics and regulatory interventions has grown. Taking, again, the example
of the UK, the AI Council (2023) lists as one of its goals: "Developing the
public understanding of AI, and tackling negative perceptions, to boost confidence of this technology among businesses and society." Although this goal
takes a more positive approach to the possibilities offered by AI than do other
(more critical) goals developed by other organisations, such goals in general
call for communicators, among others, to make specific choices. With refer-
ence to the principles developed by the UK Government, who, for instance,
decides what is fair, and how is fairness in practice to be communicated, by
whom? Do adequate ethical safeguards exist to guide such choices, or is there
more work to be done? The overall answer seems to be that, for a nascent
field confronting rapid, shape-shifting AI developments, consensus is yet to

emerge – and, as AI advances remain continuous, may never arrive – even though various proposed ground rules are on offer.

Communication professionals face an additional client-related dilemma that most (if not all) regulatory organisations do not need to consider. If AI-powered systems are intended to lead those exposed to their operations to buy a product or service, or register their support for a cause or perspective on an issue, should communicators not serve this instrumental, client-funded purpose instead of also being required to serve the social good? On this point, governments (and those they employ in communication roles) are supposed to have society's interests at their core; should their concerns supplant, or simply co-exist, with those of for-profit enterprises? That is a matter not only for individuals, professional bodies and their ethical committees to discuss, but also for national, state and local authorities – and even corporations – to consider. This is tricky territory, and there is some cynicism about the future; in an interview with Choi, an AI pioneer, Marchese (2022) asked:

> Is the ultimate hope that A.I. could someday make ethical decisions that might be sort of neutral or even contrary to its designers' potentially unethical goals – like an A.I. designed for use by social media companies that could decide not to exploit children's privacy? Or is there just always going to be some person or private interest on the back end tipping the ethical-value scale?

Choi replied: "The former is what we wish to aspire to achieve. The latter is what actually inevitably happens." As Kazim and Hilliard (2022, p. 3) point out, "[h]igh-profile examples of harm associated with algorithm failure and misuse have garnered significant public concern".

To tackle regulatory and ethics-related questions more effectively, new roles for individuals and new partnerships among groups need to be created. Kazim and Hilliard (2022, p. 4) discuss two such potentially useful roles: 'AI ethicists', academics who would educate and inform rather than lead and dictate, and 'AI ethics consultants', who would provide counsel "on AI ethics institutional strategy and even specific AI projects". In their view, "the nature of public ethics should be conducted with consensus building and inclusivity in mind" (Kazim & Hilliard, 2022, p. 3), and the debate "should not become esoteric" unless it is "by design rather than necessity" (p. 6). On this basis, interested communicators could potentially seek to facilitate the creation of AI ethics accords by working to strengthen social system interactions (see Valentini & Kruckeberg, 2011, p. 91) around AI issues. This societal-level focus is already reflected in significant national efforts to establish ethical foundations for new AI implementations. For example, Aotearoa New Zealand has a government-developed *Algorithm Charter for Aotearoa New Zealand*, whose stated aim is to help ensure that "New Zealanders have confidence in how government agencies use algorithms": a purpose that aligns with the OECD's vision of "activating" citizens as "partners to shape the future together" with government (Data.govt.nz, 2017, p. 2).

Regulatory and ethics-related developments are not just taking place in Western settings. In 2019, a collective of universities, institutes and companies in China joined under the aegis of the Beijing Academy of Artificial Intelligence (BAAI) to propose 15 principles, known as The Beijing Principles, to guide the growth of AI in China. The collective called for "the realization of beneficial AI for humankind and nature" (BAAI, 2019). Divided into three categories – research and development, use, and governance of AI – the principles include a call for "measures . . . to be taken to ensure that stakeholders of AI systems [have] sufficient informed-consent about the impact of the system on their rights and interests" (BAAI, 2019): a summons that, by implication, asks communicators to involve themselves in the effort to create and disseminate the necessary information. However, are such ethical guardrails enough, and when should they be applied (and by whom)? These questions are crucial.

Given the issues raised by AI developments, incentives (whether social or economic) need to be available in professional communication contexts to foster pre-implementation ethical reflection. The use of incentives recognises that "even as AI becomes ubiquitous, it remains an indecipherable black box for most individuals" (West, 2022, para. 5). Informed communicators might conceivably have a role in helping lay individuals decipher both whether potential benefits are being actualised and whether threatened risks are taking on substance. Yet, the matters in question relate to more than particular AI ethics predicaments limited to a single application. As Heilinger (2022, p. 1) suggests, "neglected issues of ethics and justice such as structural background injustices [should be included] into the scope of AI ethics". This call aligns with Hallahan's (2004) argument that community-building is a strong philosophy to motivate public relations practice, and Valentini et al.'s (2012, p. 873) observation that:

> the community-building theory originally espoused by Kruckeberg and Starck (1988) and modified in subsequent scholarship can provide a viable departure point toward developing new approaches to research about and practice of public relations [and]. . . that we must devise and explore new paradigms that take into account the dynamic environment wrought by changes in communication technology.

Valentini et al. are referring to the argument that Kruckeberg and Starck first advanced in 1988: that public relations is the active attempt to restore and maintain the sense of community that has been lost in contemporary society (Kruckeberg & Starck, 2004). As Valentini et al. (2012, p. 874) explain:

> Ruing this loss, they [Kruckeberg and Starck (1988) said that the Chicago School of Social Thought] sought to regain their ideal primarily through

the means by which they had perceived community to have been lost to begin with, i.e., communication – specifically the widespread use of mass media, together with easy and cheap long-distance communication among individuals, which altered people's relationships to one another.

Such an analysis aligns with the Beijing Principles' call for AI that is "beneficial AI for humankind".

Debates rage about the ways in which to foster the kinds of choices most likely to produce beneficial AI and, more fundamentally, about the very nature of beneficialness itself in relation to AI. Russell (in ITU, 2020, para. 1), in noting the current arguments about the present impossibility of making AI "good" using current AI frameworks and models, contends that: "When we talk about 'AI for good', we do not know how to define 'good' as a fixed objective in the real world that could be supplied to standard model AI systems." Even if Russell's analysis is on point, we need not abandon hope of fostering proactive choices based on the most applicable ethical standards we have, even though the technologies we are discussing have limitations. Some of these flaws – such as issues related to gender and racial bias (as previous chapters have discussed) – are especially important. For example, OpenAI's team members note that, even though OpenAI trains

> [a] class of models called Instruct GPT derived from pretrained language models such as GPT-3 . . . they sometimes fail to follow simple instructions, aren't always truthful, don't reliably refuse harmful tasks, and sometimes give biased or toxic responses.
>
> (Leike, Schulman & Wu, 2022, paras. 6–7)

Against this backdrop, communication professionals could consider resorting to some of the existing prescriptions for promoting human ethical decision-making. (See, for example, De Cremer, 2016, for suggested personal traits that may predict such behaviour; see, also, public relations-focused ethical principles, such as the Global Alliance Code of Ethics.) However, these nostrums do not cover the decisions that self-learning machines and related technologies may make autonomously. Referring to ethical dilemmas associated with digital innovation, Kane (2019, para. 3) notes that: "The mere existence of guidelines . . . doesn't guarantee [that] innovative organizations are prepared for the dilemmas they might face." Accepting his point implies that principles alone may be insufficient; this situation could create an opportunity for alert and informed communicators to help their clients and employers to navigate future troubled ethical waters. In such situations, communicators may need to rely on "algorithmic auditing" conducted by others to verify AI models, and to ascertain "whether a model complies with the values it has been intended for" (Hilliard & Gulley, 2022, paras. 10–11). The harms that such auditing could identify are not necessarily tangible; for example, according to Peltz (in Ramsey, 2023, para. 16):

> One key issue is the extent to which AI chatbots can be considered 'creators' of original content for purposes of copyright law . . . and whether such content should be entitled to the same IP protections as human creators.

Trust Issues and AI

The challenges discussed in the previous sections highlight the fact that trust becomes a key issue in considering AI ethics (as well as regulatory responses). To what extent can AI-powered output be trusted? The answer seems to resemble the proverbial curate's egg: that is, we might consider such a product partly good, and partly bad. For example, Braga and Logan (2017, p. 1) argue that "despite the usefulness of artificial intelligence . . . no computer can ever duplicate the intelligence of a human being". Yet, extensive research into human decision-making (see, for instance, Kahneman et al., 2021) has established the prevalence of cognitive biases and heuristics in decision-making, thereby positioning human choices as less rational and evidence-based than has been commonly supposed. Against this background, trust in supposedly objective AI may be seen as a sound option; however, it is one with multiple ethical implications, not least the fact that AI-enabled systems have been found to reproduce the inherent biases of the developers who provide their training data (Malik, 2022; Srinivasan & Chander, 2021). Therefore, part of the challenge for communicators is the risk that they might (even unknowingly) reproduce biased information if they lean too heavily on AI-generated content.

Other types of bias need to be taken into consideration. 'Societal AI bias' is recognised as occurring where the assumptions and norms imposed by a society generate blind spots or problematic expectations in people's thinking about AI (Correa et al., 2022). Srinivasan and Chander (2021, p. 44) point out that "biased algorithmic systems are not a new phenomenon", noting that, in 1988, a British medical school was found to have discriminated because "the algorithm used to shortlist interview candidates was biased against women and applicants with non-European names". The Public Relations Society of America identifies bias as one of the ethical issues associated with "data-driven communication"; it notes that, while such communication can be beneficial, "PR professionals may often encounter privacy issues, subjective data interpretation, algorithmic bias, unfair profiling and targeting audiences and other ethical challenges" (Ewing, 2022, para. 2).

Biases reproduce the distortions in thinking to which any human may be subject, and such distortions also apply to AI and its uses. One prime example of a distortion in thinking is the inductive bias of causality, whereby "we perceive events as contingent on other events, not merely correlated with them" (Gershman, 2021, p. 25). However, while these biases may be identified and, ideally, taken into account in human decision-making, their influence may be indiscernible; as Vaassen (2022, para. 2; original emphasis) points out:

> Many . . . AI decision algorithms are *opaque* even when they are reliable: they might deliver the right results, but they do not provide users or affected parties any insight as to how they came to produce those results.

This opacity ends up producing significant trust issues for stakeholders (and stake-seekers), who cannot always receive insights from organisations and their communicators about the exact approaches used to create AI-generated content.

The indirect swaying of choices is a significant ethical issue for communicators who wish to share messages in a principled fashion, but who themselves are fundamentally subject to these cognitive thinking distortions. One constraint is the fact that:

> academics, policymakers, and civil society organizations still lack agreement on the scope of the problems, whether they are related to technical features or historical realities, and methods for identifying and mitigating online biases – from flawed facial recognition systems to discriminatory health care algorithms.
>
> (Brookings Institution, 2019)

Any response to this dilemma (as well as related dilemmas), limited though it may be, starts with the recognition that "the future is already here – it's just in pieces" (Ball, 2022, p. 3). Responding means accepting that the multifarious applications of AI and their associated ethical predicaments cannot usefully be conceptualised or dealt with in a piecemeal fashion.

Novel Collaborations to Address Challenges

The significant, and growing, challenges being generated by AI call for novel collaborations, as well as vehicles to drive forward those collaborations, in order to develop both reactive responses and proactive tools to help address future issues successfully. Thankfully, a number of vehicles for such collaboration already exist. A prime example is the Global Alliance for Public Relations and Communication Management: a professional international association whose member organisations have over 320,000 members worldwide. The Global Alliance could help to provide the leadership and coordination necessary to develop the aforementioned ethical resources. Already, the organisation asserts that: "Ethics must be at the core of our activity. There is no public relations/ communication profession without ethics" (Global Alliance, n.d.). The Alliance, through its many members, including professional public relations institutes around the globe, has already instigated a diverse body of work focused on public relations ethics, including its own formalised code. Complementing similar standards set out by the Alliance's global PR institutional members, this code of ethics could be enhanced by the addition of AI-related components; elements to do with mitigating the effects of bias and encouraging disclosure of the design considerations employed in developing new algorithms would be particularly welcome additions. As an umbrella body with international legitimacy, both at a macro level and at a micro, local level (through individual members of the national professional associations that are part of the Global Alliance), the Alliance is well placed to orchestrate not only the enunciation of AI ethical principles, but also to provide guidance about the ways in which they can be applied in various contexts. Accepting Kazim and Hilliard's (2022, p. 8) argument that "AI ethics is public-facing in the sense that the public are the ultimate decision-makers (via a respect for their agency)", communication becomes the vehicle for their decision-making both directly (in the case of specific applications) and indirectly (through the work of independent institutions and authorities).

Additionally, beyond the Global Alliance, professional communicators – in an individual capacity – should not shy away from engaging with the fraught topic of AI regulation or governance. Lewis (2018, para. 1) notes that this type of governance helps to "close the gap . . . between accountability and ethics in technological advancement", which, Lewis explains, means determining "how much of daily life can be shaped by algorithms and who is in control of monitoring it". However, resorting to sets of ethical standards alone will fall short in the successful regulation of AI. As West (2022, para. 12) points out: "Conduct codes won't be very helpful unless they clearly delineate the scope of their coverage." Establishing clear delineation is a challenging task given the pervasiveness of AI applications. Hence, West (2022) highlights the need for 'operational tools' to enable algorithm developers to design and deploy their outputs in safe ways. The competencies required for this deployment at one time required detailed technical knowledge; now, however, "there are AI templates that bring sophisticated capabilities to people who aren't engineers or computer scientists" (West, 2022, para. 14). These templates, of course, need to be designed in ways "where their operational deployment promotes ethics and fights bias" (West, 2022, para. 15).

It seems infeasible to expect professional communicators to engage with AI development tools (and other aspects of AI more broadly) at a highly technical, detailed level; rather, communicators' role of counseling clients and employers, as well as other members of organisations (and communities), needs to include proactive advocacy for ethical and responsible AI. As part of this role, communicators need to generate sensitivity to the risks of AI (as the previous chapters have discussed). In particular, practitioners can help organisations to build and present their ethical AI-related behaviour as part of their corporate social responsibility activity. However, there is yet more to

consider. In what he calls a "constructive critique" of "the ethics of AI ethics", Heilinger (2022, p. 4) draws on the ideal of 'relational egalitarianism' to
highlight the importance of taking:

> the moral value of all human beings as the normative bedrock for ethical
> practice in all dimensions of human life and seek to secure conditions under
> which all can relate to and interact with one another on a footing of equality.

Furthermore, Heilinger (2022, p. 4) contends that bringing:

> a relational egalitarian account of justice to the normative assessment
> of AI . . . [can] expand the focus of AI ethics to pay more attention to
> the social, economic, political and environmental background structures
> within which AI is developed and used.

Professional communicators, with their understanding of the importance of
human relationships (and, by extension, the value of human beings), are ideally placed to promote relational egalitarianism in the face of AI not just in
their organisational contexts, but also in their communities.

Conclusion

Embracing proactive ethical approaches to AI is demanding because it
involves taking a broader view of the technologies and their impacts. As
Stahl (2021, p. 2) asserts: "The range of concerns [about AI] goes beyond
the immediate effects . . . on individuals [and includes] what AI could do to
humans in general." Stahl (2021, p. 3) poses the question: "[H]ow can the AI
ecosystem as a whole be shaped to foster and promote human flourishing?"
This comprehensive and nuanced perspective might be too broad to support
the specific tasks of working communicators, whose professional brief is nar-
rower; yet, engagement with ethical issues and AI is now inescapable. Those
interested in, and practicing, strategic communication face the dilemma of
how to engage, in light of the fact that adaptive and dynamic AI systems'
"past behaviors are not a perfect predictor for future behavior in identical
situations" (Stahl, 2021, p. 40). Decisions as to what to communicate, how,
and to whom must be made under conditions of considerable uncertainty. It is
at the point where uncertainty and communication need to come together that
communicators must grapple with AI ethics and their manifold implications.

References

AI Council. (2023). *AI council.* https://www.gov.uk/government/groups/ai-council
Austrian PR Ethics Council. (2017). *Ethics in digital communication.* https://iccopr.
    com/wp-content/uploads/2017/10/Ethics-in-Digital-Communications-Guidelines.pdf

BAAI. (2019). *Beijing artificial intelligence principles*. Beijing Academy of Artificial Intelligence. https://ai-ethics-and-governance.institute/beijing-artificial-intelligence-principles/

Baker, S., & Martinson, D. (2001). The TARES test: Five principles for ethical persuasion. *Journal of Mass Media Ethics, 16*(2–3), 148–175. https://doi.org/10.1080/08900523.2001.9679610

Ball, C. (2022). *Converge: A futurist's insights into the potential of our world as technology and humanity collide*. Major Street Publishing.

Borremans, P. (2023, 15 January). ChatGPT for crisis communication. *Mirror.xyz*. https://mirror.xyz/belgianbeer.eth/3GH6pTMq4ZAa6Vv3hYyoYaEi6oX1Xe5mii6mxtvms20

Braga, A. & Logan, R. K. (2017). The emperor of strong AI has no clothes: Limits to artificial intelligence. *Information, 8*(4), 1–21. https://doi.org/10.3390/info8040156

Brookings Institution. (2019, November 12). *Can algorithms alone reduce online biases?* https://www.brookings.edu/events/can-algorithms-alone-reduce-online-biases/

Correa, R., Shaan, M., Trivedi, H., Patel, B., Celi, L. A. G., Gichoya, J. W., & Banerjee, I. (2022). A systematic review of "fair" AI model development for image classification and prediction. *Journal of Medical and Biological Engineering, 42*(6), 816–827. https://doi.org/10.1007/s40846-022-00754-z

Data.govt.nz. (2017). *Algorithm charter for Aotearoa New Zealand*. https://www.data.govt.nz/toolkit/data-ethics/government-algorithm-transparency-and-accountability/algorithm-charter/

De Cremer, D. (2016, December 22). 6 traits that predict ethical behavior at work. *Harvard Business Review*. https://hbr.org/2016/12/6-traits-that-predict-ethical-behavior-at-work

Ewing, M. E. (2022, September). *Using data ethically to inform PR strategies*. Public Relations Society of America. https://www.prsa.org/article/using-data-ethically-to-inform-pr-strategies

Gershman, S. (2021). *What makes us smart: The computational logic of human cognition*. Princeton University Press.

Global Alliance. (n.d.). *Global code of ethics*. Global Alliance for Public Relations and Communication Management. https://www.globalalliancepr.org/code-of-ethics

Goldstein, J. A., Sastry, G., Musser, M., DiResta, R., Genzel, M., & Sedova, K. (2023, January). Generative language models and automated influence operations: Emerging threats and potential mitigations. *OpenAI.com*. https://cdn.openai.com/papers/forecasting-misuse.pdf

Graham, J. (2023, January 16). Artificial intelligence or abominable invention – unpicking the threats and opportunities of ai bot ChatGPT. *Comms2point0*. https://comms2point0.co.uk/comms2point0/2023/1/13/artificial-intelligence-or-abominable-invention-unpicking-the-threats-and-opportunities-of-ai-bot-chatgtpnbsp

Groll, E. (2023, January 11). Researchers: Large language models will revolutionize digital propaganda campaigns. *Cyberscoop*. https://cyberscoop.com/large-language-models-influence-operatio/

Hallahan, K. (2004). "Community" as a foundation for public relations theory and practice. *Annals of the International Communication Association, 28*(1), 233–279. https://doi.org/10.1080/23808985.2004.11679037

Heilinger, J. C. (2022). The ethics of AI ethics: A constructive critique. *Philosophy & Technology, 35*(61), 60–61. https://doi.org/10.1007/s13347-022-00557-9

Hilliard, A., & Gulley, A. (2022, December 12). What is ethical AI [blog post]. *Holistic AI.* https://www.holisticai.com/blog/ethical-ai-chat-gpt

ITU. (2020, September 29). Is 'provably beneficial' AI possible?. *ITU Hub.* International Telecommunication Union (ITU). https://www.itu.int/hub/2020/09/is-provably-beneficial-ai-possible/

Jensen, B. (2021, June 24). A new approach to mitigating AI's negative impact. *HAI: Stanford Institute for Human-Centered Artificial Intelligence.* https://hai.stanford.edu/news/new-approach-mitigating-ais-negative-impact

Kahneman, D., Sibony, O., & Sunstein, C. R. (2021). *Noise: A flaw in human judgment.* Hachette.

Kane, G. C. (2019, October 21). Establish ethical guardrails to guide digital growth. *The Wall Street Journal.* https://deloitte.wsj.com/articles/establish-ethical-guardrails-to-guide-digital-growth-01571706130

Kantrowitz, A. (2023, January 20). Why the AI ethics war will make the content moderation fight seem tame. *Big Technology.* https://www.bigtechnology.com/p/why-the-ai-ethics-war-will-make-the

Kay, J., & King, M. (2020). *Radical uncertainty.* The Bridge Street Press.

Kazim, E., & Hilliard, E. (2022, September 27). AI ethics. *Holistic AI.* https://uploads-ssl.webflow.com/6305e5d52c28356b4fe71bac/631607f844c1d2178e318475_AI%20Ethics%20White%20Paper_compressed.pdf

Kruckeberg, D. (2023, January 9). *Sailing in uncharted waters: Communications in an era of massive and insufficiently understood changes.* International Public Relations Association. https://www.ipra.org/news/itle/itl-506-sailing-in-uncharted-waters-communications-in-an-era-of-massive-and-insufficiently-understood-changes/

Kruckeberg, D. & Starck, K. (1988). *Public relations and community: A reconstructed theory.* Praeger.

Kruckeberg, D., & Starck, K. (2004). The role and ethics of community building for consumer products and services. *Journal of Promotion Management, 10*(1–2), 133–146. https://doi.org/10.1300/J057v10n01_09

Leike, J. Schulman, J. & Wu, J. (2022, August 24). Our approach to alignment research. *OpenAI Blog.* OpenAI. https://openai.com/blog/our-approach-to-alignment-research

Leslie, D. (2019). *Understanding artificial intelligence ethics and safety: A guide for the responsible design and implementation of AI systems in the public sector.* The Alan Turing Institute. https://doi.org/10.5281/zenodo.3240529

Lewis, S. (2018). AI governance. *TechTarget.* https://www.techtarget.com/searchenterpriseai/definition/AI-governance

Lindebaum, D., Glaser, V., Moser, C., & Ashraf, M. (2022, December 5). When algorithms rule, values can wither. *MIT Sloan Management Review.* https://sloanreview.mit.edu/article/when-algorithms-rule-values-can-wither/

Lipari, L. A. (2017, February 27). Communication ethics. *Oxford Research Encyclopedia of Communication.* https://doi.org/10.1093/acrefore/9780190228613.013.58

Malik, K. (2022, June 19). Forget sentience . . . the worry is that AI copies human bias. *The Guardian.* https://www.theguardian.com/commentisfree/2022/jun/19/forget-sentience-the-worry-is-that-ai-copies-human-bias

Marchese, D. (2022, December 21). An A.I. pioneer on what we should really fear. *The New York Times.* https://www.nytimes.com/interactive/2022/12/26/magazine/yeijin-choi-interview-html

Meng, J., Kim, S., & Reber, B. (2022). Ethical challenges in an evolving digital communication era: Coping resources and ethics trainings in corporate communications. *Corporate Communications, 27*(3), 581–594. https://doi.org/10.1108/CCIJ-11-2021-0128

Miles, J. (2023, January 24). What is ChatGPT and why are schools and universities so worried about students using AI to cheat? *ABC News.* https://www.abc.net.au/news/2023-01-24/what-is-chatgpt-how-can-it-be-detected-by-school-university/101884388

Ramsey, M. (2023, February 21). ChatGPT can think like a human: What are Charlotte's schools, workforce doing about AI? *The Charlotte Observer.* https://www.charlotteobserver.com/news/local/know-your-704/article271445602.html

Siau, K., & Wang, W. (2020). Artificial intelligence (AI) ethics: Ethics of AI and ethical AI. *Journal of Database Management, 31*(2), 74–87. https://dx.doi.org/10.4018/JDM.2020040105

Srinivasan, R., & Chander, A. (2021). Biases in AI systems. *Communications of the ACM, 84*(8), 44. https://doi.org/10.1145/3464903

Stahl, B. C. (2021). *Artificial intelligence for a better future: An ecosystem perspective on the ethics of AI and emerging digital technologies.* Springer. https://doi.org/10.1007/978-3-030-69978-9

UK Government. (2022). *Establishing a pro-innovation approach to regulating AI.* https://www.gov.uk/government/publications/establishing-a-pro-innovation-approach-to-regulating-ai/establishing-a-pro-innovation-approach-to-regulating-ai-policy-statement

Vaassen, B. (2022). AI, opacity, and personal autonomy. *Philosophy & Technology, 35*(88), 1–20. https://doi.org/10.1007/s13347-022-00577-5

Valentini, C. & Kruckeberg, D. (2011). Public relations and trust in contemporary global society: A Luhmannian perspective of the role of public relations. *Central European Journal of Communication, 4*(1), 91–107. https://cejc.ptks.pl/Volume-4-No-1-6-Spring-2011/Public-relations-and-trustin-contemporary-global-societyA-Luhmannian-perspective-of-t

Valentini, C., Kruckeberg, D., & Starck, K. (2012). Public relations and community: A persistent covenant. *Public Relations Review, 38*(2), 873–879. https://doi.org/10.1016/j.pubrev.2012.06.001

West, D. M. (2022, March 30). Six steps to responsible AI in the federal government: An overview and recommendations from the U.S. experience. *Brookings.* The Brookings Institution. https://www.brookings.edu/research/six-steps-to-responsible-ai-in-the-federal-government/

Summary

This chapter has canvassed some of the key ethics-related issues that communication professionals – especially in their role as critical AI activists – need to consider. In particular, the chapter has discussed the importance of the professionals taking proactive, rather than reactive, approaches to ethics. It has also highlighted the Global Alliance for Public Relations and Communication Management as an ideal vehicle for facilitating collaboration among communication practitioners to tackle issues surrounding AI ethics. As these issues grow in the future, it will become increasingly important for the practitioners to develop fresh – not to mention urgent – responses to them.

6   Conclusion

AI-related concerns, already extensive, will only continue to grow around the world in the coming years. A recent 17-country study involving over 17,000 people has revealed that only one in two employees is willing to trust AI at work (Gillespie et al., 2023). Educators and executives have shared their astonishment and alarm at the ability of the ChatGPT tool to pass exams from both law and business schools (Kelly, 2023), in addition to passing the United States Medical Licensing Examination; the Med-PaLM tool has also been found to provide medical advice almost comparable to the advice provided by a clinician (Gupta, 2023). Additionally, multiple studies have shown that, although organisations are increasingly adopting AI (and, specifically, building AI applications), only around 10 percent of organisations are succeeding in achieving superior growth and obtaining significant financial benefits from AI (Anuff, 2023; Ransbotham et al., 2020). These work-related issues, highlighting some of the most recent worries (at the time of writing) about AI, underscore individuals' and groups' more day-to-day concerns about the technologies. The more serious apprehensions relate, for example, to AI's acceleration of digital hacking and AI-enabled terrorism (Marr, 2019), as well as the reprogramming of AI tools by Internet users to produce offensive content (as in the case of DAN, short for "Do Anything Now", which was programmed by users to produce objectionable remarks) (Ali & Tong, 2023, para. 5).

Concerns about AI tools' inability to communicate as effectively as human beings will also persist in the future. Although AI's ability to perform analytical and repetitive tasks is strong, on the whole, its intuition and inference skills – crucial for communication – are far less well developed (amounting only to the capability of a nine-year-old human at best); the inability to program empathy and morality in AI successfully also exacerbates the challenges relating to communication (Orf, 2023). Chatbots, for instance, constantly make mistakes, and have been known (among other things) to give life-threatening advice, share anti-Islamic views, engage in evasion, and discriminate against minorities (Pandey, 2023). These sorts of shortcomings are compounded by AI's (current) key limitations, which include its lack of understanding of causation (that is needed in scenarios requiring the selection

DOI: 10.4324/9781003324027-6

of a best option in a series), flaws in common-sense reasoning, and its lack of human values, such as fairness and truth (Scharth, 2023a). These weaknesses highlight not just AI's limitations, but also the irreplaceability of human communication and communicators.

In light of the growing number of issues connected to AI, including communication-related concerns, this book has argued that strategic communicators should critically challenge, rather than naively champion, AI. By embracing a critical and activist role, these professional communicators would be able to help counter AI-driven threats to communities and relationships. These communicators are, collectively, in an advantageous position to counter the threats being generated by AI due to their understanding of human relationships (as well as the significance of these relationships), their relationship-building skills, and their widely recognised ability to develop, and generate engagement for, compelling messages. Communication professionals should find themselves on the front lines of the expanding battles that aim to reign in AI, mitigate the problems that it has been causing, prevent future harms, and help improve the technologies for the generations yet to come; effective communication is vital to the success of these battles, and the professionals have a crucial role to play in that respect.

Chapter by chapter, this book has outlined the ways in which strategic communicators can move from being AI champions to critical AI activists. The shift requires gaining a sound understanding of the problems connected to AI, ranging from the environmental damage it causes to its privacy-breaching mass gathering and analysis of data (as outlined in the first, introductory chapter). It also requires reflection about the problematic role that professional communicators have played to date, and still play, in encouraging the use of AI (as discussed in chapter two). Another part of communication professionals' transition from being AI backers to agitators for AI change entails understanding the value of the activist role in safeguarding relationships and communities (as chapter three explained). A range of tools has also been provided (in chapter four) to help professional communicators embrace the activist role more effectively and confront AI threats successfully. The importance of ethics – and, specifically, proactive (rather than reactive) ethics – to guide the AI-related thinking and critical actions of strategic communicators has also been highlighted (in chapter five).

Forces Pushing Against Critical AI Activism

This book acknowledges that a range of forces will push against strategic communicators' transformation into critical AI activists in the future, especially given the increasingly significant roles that AI is playing in multiple areas within our societies. New AI tools, in particular, are being developed that generate manifold benefits for individuals, groups and organisations.

For instance, new software is able to form a more accurate assessment of a cancer patient's health outlook (Millard, 2022); new satellite mapping approaches can rapidly pinpoint damage following natural disasters affecting large geographical areas (Zhu & Ye, 2022); and new astronomical systems are even detecting previously unidentified signals as part of the search for alien life (Price, 2023). Examples like these abound. The growing accessibility of, and excitement around, generative AI tools – that create text, images and other content – also represents a significant headwind for critical AI activism as individuals (including communication professionals) allow their imaginations to run wild in bringing to life content of which they had only previously dreamed. Although generative AI tools are problematic – on multiple levels (ranging from labour to ethics), and for multiple professions (such as authors and artists) – some commentators (such as Scharth, 2023b) have begun offering advice for perfecting the prompts used to create generative AI content, highlighting the growing uptake and use of these tools.

Many organisations', especially companies', increasing adoption of AI also creates challenges for the implementation of critical AI activism. Business leaders, having realised that AI can "transform corporate decision making – to increase revenue, decrease costs and improve quality" are actively sharing insights – such as the advice to automate employees' least favorite tasks – to implement AI and gain its acceptance by staff (Kellogg & Valentine, 2022, par. 1). Workers, including communicators, are much less likely to condemn AI (and much more likely to condone its use) if it makes their working lives more pleasant. Digital budgets are growing as a result; in a 2022 study of the evolving role of AI in business, 52 percent of the participating organisations reported that more than 5 percent of their digital budgets went to AI, in comparison to 40 percent of the organisations in 2018 (McKinsey & Company, 2022). In some countries, a labour and skills shortage following the COVID-19 pandemic has also resulted in AI becoming more attractive to many employers as a way of filling the void left by the unavailable workers (McKendrick, 2022).

Strategic communication teams, both in-house and client-serving, are also contending with issues that make AI use more attractive and AI activism less attractive. Budgetary limitations are a key issue, and these limitations were noted by 45 percent of the public relations professionals taking part in the State of PR 2022 survey as one of the top challenges impacting their work (Dunleavy, 2022). Communication professionals, much like business leaders, are excited about AI developments, and are providing each other with commentary about the "Transformative Powers of Artificial Intelligence for Communicators" (Elsasser, 2021). Critically-minded professional communicators will also need to continue to contend with opposition towards activism and social change in communication work. In some respects, the levels of this opposition are high; the USC Annenberg's Center for Public Relations (2022)

The Future of Corporate Activism report found that 60 percent of agencies had faced resistance from clients after recommending the incorporation of social issues into communication programs.

Implications for Policymakers and Organisational Leaders

In both the short and long terms, the implications of supporting strategic communicators in becoming AI activists would likely be highly positive for policymakers. Although research will be needed in the future to chart the implications, the communicators (as this book has discussed) would likely be able to use their specialist skills and knowledge to help publics become more aware of the issues surrounding AI; publics, in turn, would be able to take action in helping to avoid or minimise those issues (as well as exercise control over technologies) in looking after their communities, thus assisting policymakers in their efforts to contribute to the maintenance of cohesive societies. The breaking of a seven-year-old's finger by a robot in 2022 during a chess tournament threw into sharp relief the need to regulate AI more effectively; O'Sullivan (2022, pars. 15–17) points out that, although the incident during the tournament "may be seen as a once-off, it should not be ignored", given the fact that robots are being used, more and more, in "high-risk environments" that range from aged care to foundries. Stronger regulation is also needed in light of the ways in which AI can be used to generate misinformation and disinformation and, consequently, diminish trust in communities and tear the social fabric. As Stanley-Becker and Nix (2023, para. 1) have noted, generative AI's ability to create seemingly real (but actually false) imagery, which can deceive millions of people, highlights regulatory inadequacies that urgently need to be addressed; these authors rightly comment that AI's "capabilities and accessibility have vastly outpaced regulatory and legislative responses, as well as corporate controls". Hence, activism by strategic communicators would help contribute to the process of improving policymaking.

For organisational (and especially business) leaders, too, positive implications are likely to emerge from the transformation of communication professionals from AI champions to critical AI crusaders. The communicators would be able to help provide counsel that would enable organisations to undertake their AI-infused work more safely and wholesomely, thus proactively responding to AI-related issues, in addition to attempting to avoid crises. Communicators' efforts would also help organisations minimise (or even avoid) reputational damage, as well as the potential financial and legal consequences of harm brought about by AI. The activities of critical strategic communicators are all the more important in light of the finding (by Renieris et al., 2022) that managers and leaders agree that responsible AI should now be a top management concern, and that, "[f]or an organization to be a responsible AI leader, it should prioritize being more responsible in general" (Ryder, 2022, para. 6). Hence, communicators' work in relation to AI would assist efforts to implement corporate social responsibility in ways that ensure sustainability and effectively, continually involve internal organisational and external publics (Swiatek, 2023), especially given publics' ever-higher expectations for integrous organisational behaviour.

Future Research Directions

This book opens multiple avenues for further research into the ways in which strategic communicators can tackle AI threats. Future conceptual studies, in building on the conceptual research taken in the book, could explore specific communication practices for countering the threats. Practices ranging from community relations (on a broader level) to evaluation and measurement approaches (on more specific levels) could be examined. Different critical lenses for understanding the activist role could also be used in future investigations. For instance, a political economy lens would enable the power dynamics connected to the financing of AI's expansion, as well as communicators' work in challenging those power dynamics, to be scrutinised more closely. A critical race theory lens would enable the race- and ethnicity-related issues linked to AI – in addition to the work needed to be undertaken (to benefit various and presently-less-empowered ethnic and racial groups, in particular) by activist communicators – to be considered more comprehensively.

Along with conceptual research, empirical research could be undertaken to gain a stronger understanding of communication professionals' future critical AI activism. Qualitative research (using methods such as interviews and focus groups), in particular, would be helpful in gaining an understanding of communicators' perceptions of the activist role vis-à-vis AI, and the potential enablers and impediments that the professionals would face in undertaking the role. Action research could also be carried out, not just with communication professionals, but also with other publics, in order to help drive the positive, transformative change outlined in this book. Through these various research efforts, a vision of well-regulated, non-exploitative and circumscribed AI helping to maintain human relationships, as well as enabling communities to flourish, could begin to be realised in the future.

References

Ali, G., & Tong, K. (2023, March 7). Meet ChatGPT's alter ego, DAN: He doesn't care about ethics or rules. *ABC News*. https://www.abc.net.au/news/2023-03-07/chatgpt-alter-ego-dan-ignores-ethics-in-ai-program/102052338

Anuff, E. (2023, February 2). Why so many organizations' artificial intelligence initiatives fail. *The New Stack*. https://thenewstack.io/why-so-many-organizations-artificial-intelligence-initiatives-fail/

Dunleavy, K. (2022, June 2). New Muck Rack survey: The state of PR 2022. *Muck Rack*. https://muckrack.com/blog/2022/06/02/state-of-pr-2022

Elsasser, J. (2021, May 10). Exploring the transformative powers of artificial intelligence for communicators. *PR Say*. http://prsay.prsa.org/2021/05/10/exploring-the-transformative-powers-of-artificial-intelligence-for-communicators/

Gillespie, N., Curtis, C., Pool, J., & Lockey, S. (2023, February 23). A survey of over 17,000 people indicates only half of us are willing to trust AI at work. *The Conversation*. https://theconversation.com/a-survey-of-over-17-000-people-indicates-only-half-of-us-are-willing-to-trust-ai-at-work-200256

Gupta, S. (2023, February 6). What ChatGPT and other AI tools mean for the future of healthcare. *Forbes*. https://www.forbes.com/sites/forbestechcouncil/2023/02/06/what-chatgpt-and-other-ai-tools-mean-for-the-future-of-healthcare/

Kellogg, K. C., & Valentine, M. A. (2022, November 5). Five mistakes managers make when introducing AI – and how to fix them. *The Wall Street Journal*. https://www.wsj.com/articles/managers-mistakes-artificial-intelligence-11667596940

Kelly, S. M. (2023, January 26). ChatGPT passes exams from law and business schools. *CNN*. https://edition.cnn.com/2023/01/26/tech/chatgpt-passes-exams/index.html

Marr, B. (2019, August 29). What are the negative impacts of artificial intelligence (AI)? *Bernard Marr & Co*. https://bernardmarr.com/what-are-the-negative-impacts-of-artificial-intelligence-ai/

McKendrick, J. (2022, May 14). Paradox: Artificial intelligence helps solve, but suffers from skills shortages. *Forbes*. https://www.forbes.com/sites/joemckendrick/2022/05/14/paradox-artificial-intelligence-helps-solve-but-suffers-from-skills-shortages/

McKinsey & Company. (2022, December 12). *The state of AI in 2022*. Institute for Public Relations. https://instituteforpr.org/the-state-of-ai-in-2022/

Millard, E. (2022, September 1). Can AI deliver a more accurate cancer prognosis? *WebMD*. https://www.webmd.com/cancer/news/20220901/ai-cancer-prognosis

Orf, D. (2023, February 18). AI has suddenly evolved to achieve theory of mind. *Popular Mechanics*. https://www.popularmechanics.com/technology/robots/a42958546/artificial-intelligence-theory-of-mind-chatgpt/

O'Sullivan, M. (2022). A robot breaks the finger of a 7-year-old: A lesson in the need for stronger regulation of artificial intelligence. *The Conversation*. https://theconversation.com/a-robot-breaks-the-finger-of-a-7-year-old-a-lesson-in-the-need-for-stronger-regulation-of-artificial-intelligence-187612

Pandey, K. (2023, February 24). Top 5 epic fails of AI chatbots. *Jump Start*. https://www.jumpstartmag.com/top-5-epic-fails-of-ai-chatbots/

Price, D. C. (2023, January 31). AI is helping us search for intelligent alien life – and we've found 8 strange new signals. *The Conversation*. https://theconversation.com/ai-is-helping-us-search-for-intelligent-alien-life-and-weve-found-8-strange-new-signals-198754

Ransbotham, S., Khodabandeh, S., Kiron, D., Candelon, F., Chu, M., & Lafountain, B. (2020, October 20). Expanding AI's impact with organizational learning. *MIT Sloan Management Review*. https://sloanreview.mit.edu/projects/expanding-ais-impact-with-organizational-learning/

Renieris, E. M., Kiron, D., & Mills, S. (2022). To be a responsible AI leader, focus on being responsible. *MIT Sloan Management Review (and Boston Consulting Group)*. https://sloanreview.mit.edu/projects/to-be-a-responsible-ai-leader-focus-on-being-responsible/

Ryder, A. (2022, November 18). What we learned researching responsible AI this year. *MIT Sloan Management Review, Corporate Email.*

Scharth, M. (2023a, January 9). AI might be seemingly everywhere, but there are still plenty of things it can't do – for now. *The Conversation.* https://theconversation.com/ai-might-be-seemingly-everywhere-but-there-are-still-plenty-of-things-it-cant-do-for-now-197050

Scharth, M. (2023b, February 24). How to perfect your prompt writing for ChatGPT, Midjourney and other AI generators. *The Conversation.* https://theconversation.com/how-to-perfect-your-prompt-writing-for-chatgpt-midjourney-and-other-ai-generators-198776

Stanley-Becker, I., & Nix, N. (2023, March 22). Fake images of Trump arrest show "giant step" for AI's disruptive power. *The Washington Post.* https://www.washingtonpost.com/politics/2023/03/22/trump-arrest-deepfakes/

Swiatek, L. (2023). The engagement orientation and its limits in nurturing sustainability in higher education. In T. Walker, K. Tarabieh, S. Goubran & G. Machnik-Kekesi (Eds.), *Sustainable practices in higher education: Finance, strategy, and engagement* (pp. 221–238). Palgrave Macmillan. https://doi.org/10.1007/978-3-031-27807-5_11

USC Annenberg Center for Public Relations. (2022). *The future of corporate activism.* 2022 Global Communication Report. https://issuu.com/uscannenberg/docs/usc_cpr_global_communication_report_2022

Zhu, Z., & Ye, S. (2022, October 7). New satellite mapping with AI can quickly pinpoint hurricane damage across an entire state to spot where people may be trapped. *The Conversation.* https://theconversation.com/new-satellite-mapping-with-ai-can-quickly-pinpoint-hurricane-damage-across-an-entire-state-to-spot-where-people-may-be-trapped-192078

Summary

This final chapter has brought together the points made in the book about the importance of strategic communicators becoming critical AI activists instead of being advocates for AI. The need for communication professionals to take a critical stance towards AI has never been greater, and will only grow in the coming years. The chapter has acknowledged, though, that communicators face various headwinds – not just within their own (organisational) contexts, but also in society at large – in embracing this more critical role. Multiple positive implications for organisations and governments are likely to be generated by communication professionals taking a more critical approach to AI. The chapter has also outlined avenues for future research about critical AI activism on the part of strategic communicators.

Further Reading Suggestions

This short list of further reading suggestions points the way to additional sources of information about AI, activism and strategic communication not mentioned in the book. The entries in the list have been ordered alphabetically.

Chen, R. H., & Chen, C. C. (2022). *Artificial intelligence: An introduction for the inquisitive reader*. CRC Press. https://doi.org/10.1201/9781003214892

Artificial intelligence: An introduction for the inquisitive reader presents the history and development of AI. The book helpfully makes use of well-known tools involving AI – including Texas Hold'em, Deep Blue and AlphaGo – to guide readers through AI's past.

Choudry, A. (2015). *Learning activism: The intellectual life of contemporary social movements*. University of Toronto Press.

Learning activism: The intellectual life of contemporary social movements explores the intellectual life and educational work of activists. It argues that activism is best understood when it is accompanied by the learning, theorising and debating that goes with it; additionally, it highlights the collective and relational nature of activism and activist education.

Holtzhausen, D., Fullerton, J., Lewis, B. K., & Shipka, D. (2021). *Principles of strategic communication*. Routledge. https://doi.org/10.4324/9781003002048

Principles of strategic communication outlines the fundamental tenets of this type of communication. Each chapter features, among other things, a career profile of a current strategic communication professional and a current global case study.

Nothhaft, H., Werder, K. P., Verčič, D., & Zerfass, A. (2020). *Future directions of strategic communication*. Routledge. https://doi.org/10.4324/9780429295638

Future directions of strategic communication explores not only coming trends in this area of communication, but also past developments in it. The volume is divided into four parts: the emergence of the strategic communication paradigm, its conceptual foundations, the expansion of the body of knowledge, and new developments in the field.

Ricketts, A. (2012). *The activists' handbook: A step-by-step guide to participatory democracy*. Bloomsbury. http://dx.doi.org/10.5040/9781350222922

The activists' handbook: A step-by-step guide to participatory democracy provides useful approaches and tools to help citizens become involved in grassroots movements. Resources relating to both traditional or analogue and digital activism are provided. The book features case studies from the U.S., UK, Canada and Australia.

Waardenburg, L., Huysman, M., & Agterberg, M. (2021). *Managing AI wisely: From development to organizational change in practice*. Edward Elgar. https://doi.org/10.4337/9781800887671

Managing AI wisely: From development to organizational change in practice focuses on the implementation of AI in workplaces. The book uses detailed case studies of eight organisations' experiences of putting AI into effect.

Index

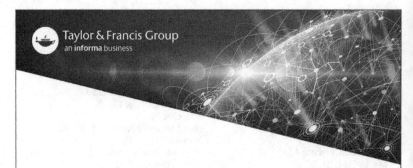

Printed in the United States
by Baker & Taylor Publisher Services